REVISE BTEC NATIONAL
Applied Law

REVISION GUIDE

Series Consultant: Harry Smith

Authors: Ann Summerscales, Richard Wortley and Nicholas Price

A note from the publisher

While the publishers have made every attempt to ensure that advice on the qualification and its assessment is accurate, the official specification and associated assessment guidance materials are the only authoritative source of information and should always be referred to for definitive guidance.

This qualification is reviewed on a regular basis and may be updated in the future. Any such updates that affect the content of this Revision Guide will be outlined at **www.pearsonfe.co.uk/BTECchanges**. The eBook version of this Revision Guide will also be updated to reflect the latest guidance as soon as possible.

For the full range of Pearson revision titles across KS2, KS3, GCSE, Functional Skills, AS/A Level and BTEC visit:
www.pearsonschools.co.uk/revise

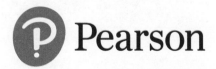

Published by Pearson Education Limited, 80 Strand, London, WC2R 0RL.

www.pearsonschoolsandfecolleges.co.uk

Copies of official specifications for all Pearson qualifications may be found on the website: qualifications.pearson.com

Text and illustrations © Pearson Education Ltd 2018
Typeset and illustrated by Kamae Design, Oxford
Produced by Out of House Publishing
Cover illustration by Eoin Coveney

The rights of Ann Summerscales, Richard Wortley and Nicholas Price to be identified as authors of this work have been asserted by them in accordance with the Copyright, Designs and Patents Act 1988.

First published 2018

23
10 9 8 7 6

British Library Cataloguing in Publication Data
A catalogue record for this book is available from the British Library

ISBN 978 1 292 22165 6

Acknowledgements
The authors and publisher would like to thank the following individuals and organisations for permission to reproduce copyright material:

Photographs
(Key: b-bottom; c-centre; l-left; r-right; t-top)

Alamy Stock Photo: Ian Marlow iii, 28, Kzenon 09, Gavin Rodgers/Pixel 8000 Ltd 12, Greg Balfour Evans 13, Illia Uriadnikov 16, Ian Macpherson London 19, Tom Wood 27, Shaun A Daley 29, Gordon Shoosmith 32l, Cliff Hde Local 32r, Uknip 33, Lebrecht Music and Arts Photo Library 48, Image Source Plus 54, Brian Harris 58, Chris Brignell 66b, Sebastian Remme 69, Photofusion Picture Library 71, Michael Kemp 75, 67photo 78, Cultura Creative (RF) 79; **Press Association:** PA Archive 20; **Reuters:** Handout 64; **Shutterstock:** Designer491 05, SpeedKingz 06, Richie Chan 08, Wutzkohphoto 17, Lals Stock 22, Pressmaster 25l, Dmitry Skutin 25r, Unguryanu 31, Sergey Nivens 36, WDG Photo 61, Rawpixel.com 66t

All other images © Pearson Education

Text
Page 52: (2013) 177 JPN Issue 25. https://www.criminallawandjustice.co.uk/features/Theft-%E2%80%93-Simple-Offence-Ov ercomplicated Published by LexisNexis UK.

Page 96: Reproduced with the permission of Woodfines LLP.

Notes from the publisher
1. While the publishers have made every attempt to ensure that advice on the qualification and its assessment is accurate, the official specification and associated assessment guidance materials are the only authoritative source of information and should always be referred to for definitive guidance.

Pearson examiners have not contributed to any sections in this resource relevant to examination papers for which they have responsibility.

2. Pearson has robust editorial processes, including answer and fact checks, to ensure the accuracy of the content in this publication, and every effortismadetoensur e this publication is free of e rrors. We are, however, only human, and occasionally errors do occur. Pearson is not liable for any misunderstandings that arise as a result of errors in this publication, but it is our priority to ensure that the content is accurate. If you spot an error, please do contact us at resourcescorrections@pearson.com so we can make sure it is corrected.

Websites
Pearson Education Limited is not responsible for the content of any external internet sites. It is essential for tutors to preview each website before using it in class so as to ensure that the URL is still accurate, relevant and appropriate. We suggest that tutors bookmark useful websites and consider enabling students to access them through the school/college intranet.

Introduction

Which units should you revise?

This Revision Guide has been designed to support you in preparing for the externally assessed units of your course. Remember that you won't necessarily be studying all the units included here – it will depend on the qualification you are taking.

BTEC National qualification	Externally assessed units
Certificate	1 Dispute Solving in Civil Law
Extended Certificate	1 Dispute Solving in Civil Law 3 Applying the Law

Your Revision Guide

Each unit in this Revision Guide contains two types of pages, shown below.

Content pages help you revise the essential content you need to know for each unit.

Skills pages help you prepare for your exam or assessed task. Skills pages have a coloured edge and are shaded in the table of contents.

Use the **Now try this** activities on every page to help you test your knowledge and practise the relevant skills.

Look out for the **example student responses** to exam questions or set tasks on the skills pages. Post-its will explain their strengths and weaknesses.

Contents

A small bit of small print
Pearson publishes Sample Assessment Material and the Specification on its website. This is the official content and this book should be used in conjunction with it. The questions in *Now try this* have been written to help you test your knowledge and skills. Remember: the real assessment may not look like this.

The features of civil law

Civil law is a separate system from criminal law. It deals with disputes between individuals or businesses. The main aim of civil law is to regulate business and personal life and to provide a remedy (in the form of financial compensation) if there is a dispute, or if someone is at fault causing loss or injury to another person. Unlike criminal law, the aim is **not** punishment of an individual through imprisonment or community service.

The aim and purpose of civil law

Civil law covers many areas of life.

Burden of proof

Evidence must be presented to the court to show why the claimant should win their case. In civil cases, the burden of proof will be on the injured claimant to show why they have an arguable case.

Standard of proof

Civil law has a lower level of proof than criminal law as the aim of civil law is compensation – not to punish the defendant. By comparison, a case against a defendant in a criminal case must be proved beyond reasonable doubt.

The claimant has to prove their case on **the balance of probabilities** – the judge has to be over 50 per cent sure that the defendant is liable.

Now try this

Make a list of the types of evidence that could be used in court to support a claim for personal injury damages.

Civil court hierarchy

If the parties to a dispute cannot settle it themselves, they may have to go to court for a resolution to be imposed on them.

Trial courts

Civil trials take place in either the **County Court** or **High Court** depending on the amount being claimed. These are the only courts that hear an initial trial so they are known as **courts of first instance**.

The claim will set out the grounds and amount of the claim. A defence may be filed by the defendant who is being sued. The case will be heard and decided by a judge. There is normally no jury.

- Claims below £100,000 are usually heard in the County Court.
- Claims over £100,000 are usually heard in the High Court.
- Claims in contract and tort law will be heard in the Queen's Bench Division of the High Court.

Civil court hierarchy

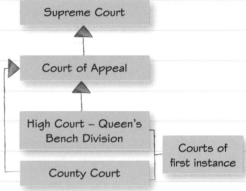

Tort law

This is the part of civil law that deals with civil wrongs, such as negligence.

Contract law

This is the part of civil law serving to protect people and businesses who have made agreements relating to goods and services.

Juries in civil cases

The County Courts Act 1984 established guidelines for when a jury should be used for a civil trial. This includes cases involving:

- ☑ libel or slander
- ☑ malicious prosecution
- ☑ false imprisonment
- ☑ fraud.

A judge can refuse a trial by jury if they believe the case too complex for trial by jury.

Tracks

Civil courts operate a tracking system to allocate cases to the correct track to ensure they are dealt with efficiently and within specific time limits. Judges can manage the way the case should be dealt with.

Tracking system

- Small claims track – for disputes under £10,000 or £1000 in personal injury claims
- Fast-track – for claims between £10,000 and £25,000
- Multi-track for claims over £25,000

The trial

The parties can represent themselves or use barristers or solicitors to act on their behalf. Most evidence will be filed before the hearing but some oral evidence can be given. The judge will decide who wins the case on the balance of probabilities and any damages and costs to be paid.

Appeals

Either party can appeal to the Court of Appeal against the liability or amount of damages. This must be made within 21 days after the date of the decision of the lower court.

Permission will not be given for an appeal unless it is likely to succeed, for example if the Court of Appeal believes the decision of the lower court was wrong or unjust because of serious irregularities. There are relatively few appeals each year.

A further appeal can be made to the Supreme Court but only on issues of law of national importance.

Now try this

Jill is injured in a car accident due to the fault of a motorcyclist, Ben. She has suffered serious injuries and damage to her car. Jill wants to claim compensation of around £10,000 and to know which court could deal with her claim. Outline what Jill would have to do before she starts her court claim, and explain how the amount of damages indicates which court would be used.

Role of judges in civil courts

Some civil disputes can be settled between the parties themselves and never need to go to court. However, when disputes do get taken to court, a judge will decide who wins a civil dispute and the parties will have to accept the judge's decision.

A civil courtroom

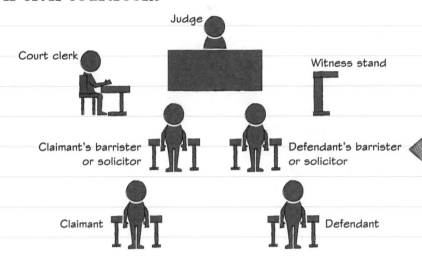

In a civil courtroom the parties (both claimant and defendant) can have a lawyer to represent them or they can represent themselves. Both solicitors and barristers are types of lawyer.

Case management

The judge has complete control of the case to:

- encourage the parties to cooperate with each other.
- help them to agree a settlement.
- encourage them to use **alternative dispute resolution (ADR)**.
- control the progress of the case.
- decide which witnesses are needed.

The trial

At the trial the judge will:

- read the case papers before the hearing.
- hear any evidence from witnesses and legal arguments during the hearing.
- decide who is liable considering any **precedent**.
- decide the amount of **damages** to be paid.
- decide who pays the costs.

Damages and costs

The main purpose of bringing a civil claim is to obtain financial compensation to make good the loss or injury that has been suffered. The judge will decide the amount of damages based on the severity of injuries or amount of loss.

In a civil case, the general rule is 'the loser pays the winner's legal costs' as well as their own. The exception is the small claims court in which you can only claim certain costs.

Know your terms

ADR: alternative dispute resolution – ways of resolving a case without going to court

Precedent: previously decided case that set out rules which a judge may have to follow

Damages: amounts of money payable by the loser of a civil claim to compensate the victim

🔗 **Links**   For more on ADR, see pages 4–7. For more on judicial precedent, see page 22, and for more on damages, see page 36.

Now try this

Is the rule that the loser pays the winner's legal costs an incentive or disincentive to taking court action? Give reasons for your answer.

Consider the alternatives to litigation.

Negotiation and ombudsmen

Negotiation is the most informal way of settling a dispute. If this does not work, and the other party is a member of a trade association, it may be possible to use an ombudsman to settle a dispute.

Negotiation

Negotiation can be carried out in many ways. The aim is to find a resolution that is acceptable to both parties.

Talking on the phone

Exchanging written messages – letter or emails

Getting a representative, such as a union representative, to talk for you

Negotiation – the first stage in dealing with any dispute

Face to face

Getting a lawyer to deal with the other party or with their lawyer

An example of a provider: Watts & Co, a local electrician

An example of a trade association: Electrical Contractors Association

An example of an ombudsman: The Consumer Ombudsman

Ombudsman services

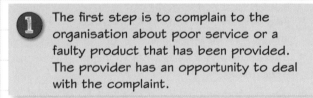

1 The first step is to complain to the organisation about poor service or a faulty product that has been provided. The provider has an opportunity to deal with the complaint.

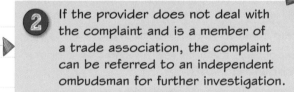

2 If the provider does not deal with the complaint and is a member of a trade association, the complaint can be referred to an independent ombudsman for further investigation.

4 Following investigation, the ombudsman will announce a decision. If in favour of the consumer, the service provider should act on the decision. If in favour of the provider, the consumer has no appeal or right to take further action.

3 The service will be free to the consumer. The ombudsman will investigate the complaint by contacting both parties for their version of the events.

Now try this

Asha is unhappy with the double glazing she has had installed. She has dealt with a firm that is a member of a trade association. Write a list of bullets points to explain to her how her dispute could be dealt with.

Arbitration

Arbitration is a way of dealing with a dispute instead of it being decided in court. This happens when there is an artibration clause in a contract between the parties.

The arbitrator

Arbitration is a form of alternative dispute resolution in which an arbitrator settles a dispute between two parties.

An arbitrator will be an expert in the subject of the dispute, and has had formal training in arbitration. Many, but not all, arbitrators are lawyers.

The process

The parties will always set out their cases in a written statement. Oral evidence may also be called for.

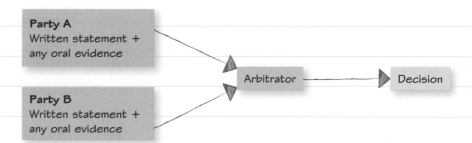

Party A
Written statement + any oral evidence

Party B
Written statement + any oral evidence

Arbitrator

Decision

When does arbitration occur?

There will be a written contract between the parties. One of the terms will be a clause which sets out that, if there is a dispute, it will be resolved by arbitration rather than going to court. An example of a clause in the contract could be:

'Any dispute or difference arising out of or in connection with this contract shall be decided by a single arbitrator who is to be agreed between the parties, or failing agreement to be appointed by the President of the Chartered Institute of Arbitrators.'

Some arbitration schemes are free. It is usually still cheaper than going to court even if fees are charged.

The decision

The arbitrator:
- will decide the case on the evidence that has been produced.
- is unlikely to follow any precedent.
- can set the amount of any compensation that has to be paid.

Appeals

The arbitrator's decision will be final and the parties will not be able to appeal or to take the case to court.

The parties may be required to each pay a proportion of the arbitrator's costs.

Now try this

Nick has been on a package holiday but is unhappy with the hotel and its facilities as they were not as described in the brochure. He wants compensation but finds an arbitration clause in the small print. He wants to know what it means. Write some notes for Nick to help explain the effect of the clause and the process of arbitration.

Consider who your audience is. Your notes need to be accessible to someone who has no knowledge of the law.

Conciliation and mediation

Conciliation and mediation are similar ways of solving a dispute but are used in different situations. An expert is called upon to help the parties reach a settlement.

Conciliation

Conciliation will often be used in a dispute between a consumer and a retailer or supplier, or in workplace situations.

An independent conciliator can be asked by either party to help.

Advisory Conciliation and Advisory Service (ACAS) will become involved in employment claims and disputes to attempt early settlement.

| An impartial expert conciliator sits down with both parties, in the same room, in an informal setting. |

↓

| The conciliator helps both parties talk to each other. |

↓

| The conciliator can make suggestions and lead discussions to help reach a settlement. |

↓

| Once an agreement acceptable to both parties is reached, it can be written down to become formal. |

Mediation

An impartial trained mediator will help the parties maintain their relationship and reach a settlement – whether it is business or personal.

The process will be voluntary and confidential.

| An impartial trained mediator will work with the parties but they do not have to meet face to face and will often be in separate rooms or buildings. |

↓

| The mediator will 'shuttle' between the parties, conveying messages and offers to settle the dispute. |

↓

| Mediators can put forward suggestions but they don't make judgements or decide the outcome. |

↓

| Agreement is reached when there is common ground between the parties. |

↓

| Once agreement is reached it may be formalised in writing. |

Costs

- Conciliators charge by the hour. The amount they charge may depend on how complex the case is and how long it takes to deal with.
- Mediators charge by the hour. If their fees are agreed using the scale on the government website, they will be fixed based on the amount being claimed.

Family mediation is often used to help to settle family disputes where the relationship between the parties is sensitive, especially if children are involved.

Now try this

Josh is having issues at work with both his employer and some fellow workers. He has been offered both conciliation and mediation to try to resolve the issues. He is undecided which approach to use as he wants to continue working for the firm. Briefly explain the similarities and differences between these two methods of dispute resolution.

Alternative dispute resolution (ADR)

Using the civil courts is the traditional way of solving a civil dispute. However, because of problems with using the courts, alternative methods of dispute resolution have become more popular.

Precedent – judges must follow strict rules of precedent to decide result.

Links See pages 4–6 for information on different forms of ADR.

Cost – lawyers' fees; loser pays winner's legal costs, as well as their own.

Complexity of rules of procedure and language – failure to follow correct procedure may mean loss of the case.

Problems with using civil courts

Result – there must be a winner and a loser in every case with little room for compromise.

Delay – lengthy court cases and hearings plus possibility of more than one hearing.

Adversarial – court hearings do not always consider all the evidence; lawyers may rely on strength of argument and persuasion to win their case.

Advantages of ADR

There can be good reasons to opt for ADR above taking a case to court.

👍 Quicker and cheaper – fixed dates can usually be arranged; there is no need for lawyers to be involved.

👍 Procedures – there are few strict rules of procedure; meetings and any hearings are informal.

👍 Expertise – those carrying out ADR are likely to be experts in their field of dispute resolution and the subject of the dispute.

👍 Solutions – ADR aims to provide a resolution or settlement that is acceptable to both parties.

Disadvantages of ADR

While ADR can be a good alternative to the courts, it can have its drawbacks.

👎 Predictability – it may be difficult to predict the result of the dispute as each case is settled on its own facts and there is no precedent to follow.

👎 Legal expertise – as lawyers are not used, there may be a dispute interpreting the wording of clauses or contracts.

👎 Enforcement – any settlement reached may have to be applied or enforced, which may involve further delay or difficulty.

👎 Solutions – if settlement is not reached or not possible, the case may still have to go to court.

Now try this

You bought from a jeweller's shop an expensive watch which does not work properly. The shop tells you to contact the manufacturer who tells you to deal with the shop. Make a list of points for and against using ADR to resolve this dispute as opposed to taking the manufacturer or the shop to court.

Legal sources

An important skill for a lawyer is to find and use valid sources of law to support an argument and to find out the current state of the law.

Legislation

This is law passed by Parliament and is the highest form of law. It is also known as **primary legislation**.

Legislation.gov.uk aims to publish legislation within 24 hours of its availability in print. Some more complex documents may take longer to prepare. Where legislation is not available on this website, you may find a copy in a law or university library or at a major public library.

 Links   All laws passed by Parliament can be found at www.legislation.gov.uk.

If a law is called an **Act of Parliament** it means that the law has been passed by Parliament and the content of an Act can be quoted, and has to be accepted, as an authoritative source of law.

A lawyer will have to check that the law is in force and that it has not been amended (changed) by a later Act.

Delegated legislation

Laws drafted by government ministers and approved by Parliament are one form of delegated legislation. They are known as Statutory Instruments.

They can be used to bring into force the whole or part of an Act of Parliament or to fill in the detail in an Act.

When using delegated legislation, its full name, number and year it was passed should be referred to.

A lawyer should check that the delegated legislation is in force and that it has not been amended by any later law. It has to be accepted in the same way as primary legislation.

Statutory interpretation

Sometimes the meaning of a word or words in a piece of legislation is not clear. Lawyers cannot go back to Parliament to ask for the meaning so it is for the courts to interpret and give a meaning to the words.

Courts interpret primary legislation created by the Houses of Parliament.

Judicial precedent

These are decisions of judges in court – the higher the court, the greater the authority of the precedent.

At the end of a civil case, a judge will set out the finding of facts, summarise the relevant law and apply the law to the facts. This precedent should then be followed in subsequent cases.

Now try this

You are working in a law firm and you have been asked by your firm's principal to find out the law on a case for a client. Before you start your research, make a plan for how you are going to find out the relevant law.

Methods of appropriate professional communication

It is essential that lawyers can communicate effectively both orally and in writing with their clients, other lawyers and before courts and tribunals. This spider diagram shows some of the things a client might be concerned about, and which a lawyer should be aware of when communicating with their client.

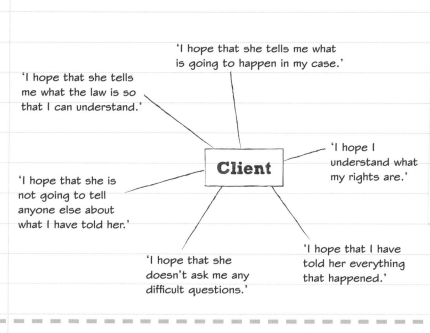

'I hope that she tells me what is going to happen in my case.'

'I hope that she tells me what the law is so that I can understand.'

'I hope that she is not going to tell anyone else about what I have told her.'

Client

'I hope I understand what my rights are.'

'I hope that she doesn't ask me any difficult questions.'

'I hope that I have told her everything that happened.'

Communications between lawyer and client are **privileged**, meaning that the lawyer should not tell anyone else what has been disclosed.

Other solicitors

A lawyer will have to put their client's case, together with the reasons for making the claim or defending the claim, to other lawyers.

They may have to negotiate a settlement with another lawyer or insurance company on behalf of their client.

Barristers

A solicitor may have to ask a barrister for advice about a case or to request the barrister to draft case papers. The brief to the barrister will have to be clear on what has happened, the issues and arguments in the case and what the barrister is being requested to produce.

 Links Revise brief to counsel on page 11.

Courts and tribunals

Before trial the lawyer will have to make sure the correct forms are completed to show the reasons for a claim or a valid defence.

At the hearing the lawyer will also have to:

- dress appropriately
- use correct language to address the judge, other lawyers and witnesses
- present their case effectively and accurately

- show respect to the judge – agree or disagree with their opinion, giving reasons for their view
- show respect to witnesses when questioning them
- respect the final decision.

Now try this

Think about a client's legal understanding, and general court processes.

Outline potential issues if communication is poor between a lawyer and client, or in a court hearing.

Solicitors' letters

When solicitors are acting for parties to a case, they communicate with each other using special conventions and terminology.

Give the address and contact details of the firm sending the letter at the top right.

Personal Injury Solicitors

Garden House
Kings Meadow
Brighton BN1
Tel 01632 960960
Email: pisolicitors@link.com
Website: www.pisolicitors

8 August 2017

Dear Sirs

We have been instructed by Julian Norris of 1 Green Road, Brighton. We understand Mr Norris was involved in an accident at work in which he was seriously injured. We understand that you act for his employers, Image.

We are informed that Mr Norris was injured when the ceiling of his office collapsed on top of him, trapping him at his desk and causing his right hand to be crushed underneath his computer. Our client has suffered both physical and psychological injuries as a result of this experience, which was entirely the fault of your clients.

We have advised Mr Norris that he is entitled to claim substantial compensation for his injuries. Unless your clients are prepared to offer appropriate compensation to our client within the next seven days we are instructed to issue court proceedings. Please advise us whether you have instructions to accept service of any court proceedings.

Yours faithfully

Personal Injury Solicitors

To:
G. Brown & Co Solicitors
1 Seafront
Brighton

In the first letter, always state the name and address of the person the firm is acting for.

Briefly state what has happened and outline the injuries suffered to clarify the reason for the letter, and emphasise the severity of the case. More detail can be included in later letters.

Make it clear from the start who is to blame for the accident and injuries.

Be clear in what you are asking and any time limit for responding.

Use legal terminology, for example 'accept service of court proceedings', meaning that a lawyer is authorised to proceed with the next steps of the case.

The addressee's details go on the left-hand side of the letter.

 Links   Look at page 46 to revise the format and features of solicitors' letters.

Now try this

Write a follow-up letter to the letter above sending the claim form.

Assume there has been no reply to the letter above.

Brief to counsel

When a solicitor briefs a barrister (who is known as 'counsel'), they are providing details as to what they are expected to do if they are appearing in court. A solicitor may also 'instruct' a barrister. This is when they require the barrister's opinion on a specific case.

In the High Court of Justice
Queen's Bench Division

Case No 01 of 2017

BETWEEN

John Smith

v

ABC Recycling Co

BRIEF TO COUNSEL

Instructing solicitors act on behalf of John Smith who has suffered a serious eye injury at work.

Our client was gravely injured at work when a sharp piece of plastic struck our client in the left eye, piercing his eyeball. We consider that the accident was completely the fault of the employers as our client was not supplied with appropriate goggles and an unsafe system of work was being followed. Our client's statement about the accident and a copy of the health and safety report are enclosed with this brief.

A copy of a medical report is also enclosed confirming the surgery carried out. It shows there has been some improvement in the vision but it will never be the same as it was before the accident.

Negotiations have taken place with the employer but no agreeable settlement has been reached.

Counsel is requested to:

1. advise on the likely success of court proceedings for negligence against Mr Smith's employers;

2. advise on the likely compensation that could be achieved. We consider that a claim should be made for damages for the injury, as well as medical expenses, loss of earnings and the care and assistance he received following the accident;

3. draft a statement of claim to be issued to start the court proceedings.

Personal Injury Solicitors
Garden House
Kings Meadow
Brighton BN1
Tel 01632 960960

 Head up instructions with details of the court and the parties.

Include copies of relevant documents such as court papers, correspondence, contracts, medical reports or details of losses or injuries, together with any statement of facts from the client or witnesses.

Clearly set out what the barrister is being asked to do – for example, give an opinion as to the law, draft some legal documents and/or appear at court.

Name and address of the firm of solicitors sending the Brief to Counsel

Now try this

 Assume the claim has been defended.

Draft a further brief instructing counsel to appear at the trial in court.

11

Advice from solicitors and barristers

If you are injured in an accident you may think of approaching a legal adviser for advice and help with making a claim. There are different types of legal adviser who may be able to help.

Solicitors

- Have offices in most towns and cities and have direct contact with their clients.
- Will be able initially to advise whether a claim is likely to be successful.
- Can help obtain evidence and reports, such as accident and medical reports, and draft the claim to be issued in court.
- Hold confidential discussions with their clients.
- Are governed by strict rules of conduct and regulated by the Law Society.

Claims and solicitors' fees

If the claim is for:

- a small amount, they may be able to do the advocacy in court.
- a larger amount, they may suggest instructing a barrister to deal with the advocacy.
- Solicitors will either be paid:
  - on a 'no win no fee' basis (in which case they must be sure that the case stands a strong chance of succeeding), or
  - a rate based on the amount of time they spend on the case.

Links See page 15 to revise private funding and funding own insurance.

Barristers

- Will usually be contacted via a solicitor but in civil accident claims they can be contacted directly by a client through the 'Direct access' scheme.
- Work from chambers situated in larger towns and cities and usually specialise in one area of law.
- Will be able to advise on the likely success of a claim, draft a claim form and carry out advocacy in court.
- May ask the client to obtain reports and evidence and issue the court papers.
- Will usually be paid a fixed fee based on the amount of work they are likely to carry out and time spent on the case.

Barristers' advocacy in court is governed by rules of conduct and procedure. They are regulated by the Bar Council.

Legal executives

- Are usually employed by a solicitor to obtain evidence for a case and to draft case papers.
- Can carry out some advocacy and appear in hearings to plan future directions of smaller cases.
- Will be paid a salary by a solicitor.

Paralegals

- Will usually be employed by a solicitor to obtain evidence for the case, interview witnesses and to draft the case papers.
- Will support a barrister in any court hearings.
- Will be paid a salary by a solicitor.

Now try this

Dean was involved in an accident at work and has been told by a friend to seek legal advice. He has never had to use a lawyer before and wants to know what each type of legal adviser does. Make some notes to help him decide who to approach about a possible claim.

Advice from Citizens Advice and Law Centres

You can go to Citizens Advice or a Law Centre for advice if you are involved in a dispute and cannot afford, or do not know, a lawyer to advise you.

Citizens Advice

Citizens Advice is a national charity offering free, impartial and confidential advice and guidance on a range of issues and problems – not just legal. They provide face-to-face meetings at over 3000 locations across the UK.

Pro bono means 'for the public good', so solicitors and barristers and law students work as volunteers, for no charge. This is usually for people who need legal assistance but who cannot afford to pay for support.

Citizens Advice:

* offer advice and assistance on a range of civil cases.
* permit lawyers to attend meetings to provide more specialist advice.
* can write letters on behalf of and complete forms for clients.
* can negotiate on behalf of clients.
* can refer more complicated disputes to a local lawyer.
* operate a comprehensive website giving advice on a range of consumer issues.

Law Centres

Law Centres support people who cannot afford legal representation. There is a national network but each centre operates individually.

Law Centres:

* must fundraise and obtain grants for continued funding.
* are often located in less affluent towns and cities.
* use lawyers who may work *pro bono* or as part of work experience.
* can offer initial advice on a range of civil matters and on specialist issues such as housing and immigration.
* may be prepared to pursue a full case for a client and represent them before court or tribunal.

Citizens Advice in action

Patrick is visually impaired. He took out a loan when he was working full time but was made redundant and could only get part-time work. He could not keep up his loan payments.

Citizens Advice drew up a financial statement and negotiated with the loan company to reduce the payments to an amount he could afford. Interest payments and charges were also frozen.

Law Centres at work

Shanaz was facing eviction from her temporary accommodation which would have left her homeless. She was suffering severe mental health problems.

The Law Centre managed to obtain legal funding and defended the court case on the grounds that Shanaz had no mental capacity to litigate and that this was a breach of the Equality Act.

A settlement was reached for the action to be dropped, costs were recovered and the Centre is working to get her rehoused.

Now try this

Anya needs advice about a possible civil claim she wants to make. She wants advice about whether to approach Citizens Advice or a Law Centre. Outline the different matters she will have to consider before she decides which sources of advice to approach.

Advice from insurance companies and online

Insurance companies can offer legal advice or representation. You can also get free legal advice from online sources.

Insurance companies

When you take out an insurance policy, for example for a car or for your house and its contents, the insurance company will often offer you extra insurance to cover any legal expenses you might incur.

If you make an insurance claim that leads to any kind of legal dispute, the company will instruct a solicitor on your behalf and meet their fees.

Policies like this are usually optional and they will cost you – but they can save you a lot of money if you face solicitors' or barristers' fees in the future.

The internet

You can find a wealth of advice on legal matters on the internet. However, you must be certain that the advice is accurate and that the website offers advice based on English law rather than, for example, US law or Scottish law.

 The Law Society offers reliable advice: www.lawsociety.org.uk.

Easy to access

Will specialise in certain types of claim

Advantages of legal advice from insurance companies

Company can instruct high-quality advisers/lawyers

No extra payment required by insured

Information available immediately

Wide range of information on offer

Free

Advantages of legal advice from the internet

Publicity may encourage provider to settle early

May find others with similar problems to share experiences

Must pay for policy, even if no claim made

Advice cannot be given face to face

Disadvantages of legal advice from insurance companies

Legal support can be limited – some situations might not be covered

You cannot choose who will represent you

Law may not be England– or Wales –based (Scottish law can be different)

Information or advice may be inaccurate

Disadvantages of legal advice from the internet

Partial advice unless you sign up or subscribe

Now try this

Consider who is giving or receiving the advice.

Add one extra point to each of the spider diagrams on this page.

Funding your own legal costs

If a person wants legal advice or help, they can pay for it themselves, potentially using a 'no win no fee' arrangement or using an insurance policy.

Paying fees

If someone can pay their own legal fees, then they are able to choose the best legal service for their needs, providing flexibility and benefits.

👍 The person can choose how much they want to pay in total.

👍 The person can negotiate a fee with a lawyer.

👍 The lawyer will charge based on an hourly rate multiplied by the amount of time spent on the case.

👍 If the person wins the case they can often recover the amount of the costs they have paid out in addition to the compensation.

'No win no fee' arrangements

This is also known as a **conditional fee arrangement** (CFA) and splits the financial risk of a legal case between the lawyer and the client.

A lawyer may be willing to offer a no win no fee arrangement for a client.

- The lawyer may carry out initial work to assess the chances of the case succeeding.
- The client will sign an agreement with the lawyer.
- The lawyer may require the client to take out an insurance policy to cover the costs if the case is unsuccessful.
- The lawyer will need to be satisfied that the case has a good chance of success – better than 75%.
- If the lawyer accepts the case they will bear the costs of the case and not charge the client unless the case is won and compensation is obtained.

- The lawyer will fight the case and attempt to win compensation for the client.
- If the case is won, the lawyer will be able to claim their costs from the loser in addition to any compensation.
- If the case is lost the lawyer will not charge the client and will have to bear the costs of the case themselves or claim them from the insurance company.

Insurance policies

It is possible to take out insurance which covers legal fees. However, any insurance policy will contain much small print that should be read and understood as this may limit or exclude the cover available for legal fees. An example of such a clause is: '*the maximum benefit for legal fees that we will pay under this policy following a motoring accident is £50,000 if cover A has been selected or £100,000 if cover B has been selected.*'

Before the event insurance policy

The client buys a policy before suffering an accident. The policy contains a clause agreeing to pay legal costs if an accident takes place later. This is the most popular type of insurance policy.

After the event insurance policy

The client buys an insurance policy after suffering an accident. The policy contains a clause agreeing to pay the legal costs if a claim is made.

> If a client has limited experience of the law, like Javed, remember to explain clearly any legal terminology you need to use.

Now try this

Javed wants to claim compensation for injuries he has suffered in an accident. He has seen adverts about 'no win no fee' deals. He wants to know more about them and whether he can use this type of arrangement to cover his legal costs. Write an email to Javed outlining CFAs and explain how they work.

Funding by trade unions and the state

Funds for legal advice and representation may be provided by the state in some instances. Trade unions will also meet some legal costs.

Trade union

If you are involved in a civil dispute, and you are a member of a trade union, you may receive help and advice as a benefit of being a union member.

> Individual pays subscriptions and is a member of a trade union.

| Member requires advice on an issue with their employer. | Union officials can offer initial advice to member. | Union officials can contact and negotiate with employer on behalf of member. | More complicated issues can be referred to union's legal department for advice and assistance. | Union official or lawyer can represent member before tribunal or court. | If claim is successful, member will receive full compensation without deduction. |

State funding

Some legal cases can be paid for with state funding (funding from the government). This is known as legal aid. However, due to the high cost to the government of legal aid, there are very strict criteria as to who is eligible to receive it. It can be entirely free but sometimes a client has to make a contribution.

Legal aid may help to pay for legal services for problems such as housing, debt and family matters.

Types of legal aid

Different types of legal aid include:

- ✓ legal help and family help – advice on rights and help to negotiate and draw up agreements.
- ✓ help at court – where someone speaks on the client's behalf at court.
- ✓ family mediation – to resolve a family dispute after a relationship has broken down (without going to court). It can help to resolve problems involving children, money and the family home.

> If legal aid is available for the type of dispute, an organisation offering it must have a contract with the Legal Aid Agency. Legal aid may be available through solicitors, Law Centres and some Citizens Advice offices.

Now try this

Because of his work Brian is a member of a trade union. He thinks his employer has wrongfully discriminated against him by refusing him promotion. Outline where he could get advice and explain how he could be helped to make a claim against his employer.

Costs in taking legal action

If a case has to go to court there will be a number of possible costs involved, some of which will have to be paid up front. Others may be claimed at the end of the case. It can be very expensive to take a case to court and that is why people are strongly encouraged to consider alternative methods of resolving a dispute. The main areas of cost are listed below.

 Court fees

In order to issue a case in court, an initial fee has to be paid to the court.

The fee amount will depend on the type of case, the court it is issued in and the amount of the claim.

If the claim can be issued online, the court fee may be cheaper.

More fees may be payable for further court hearings.

 Legal representation

If a lawyer is needed to present (or defend) a court action, fees will be payable based on the time involved and the complexity of the case.

- A solicitor will be paid an hourly fee multiplied by the time spent on the case.
- It may be possible to negotiate a fixed fee if a barrister is required for advice or court presentation.

③ Awarding of costs

The rule in civil cases is that the winner's costs are paid by the loser, plus any compensation. The loser has to pay for their own costs too – except in a small claims court. This can act as a deterrent to taking court action (it can put people off going to court).

 Links See page 1 for a reminder of the aims of civil law.

④ Compensation

The loser of a court action may be required to pay compensation to the winner. This may have to be paid immediately or in instalments.

Losing a legal case can have serious financial consequences.

Hidden costs

- 👎 The ability of the loser to pay compensation and costs can only be investigated following judgment – they may not be able to pay.
- 👎 Further costs may be incurred in forcing the loser to pay compensation and costs.
- 👎 An individual's or business's reputation may be damaged by the publicity of taking or defending court action.
- 👎 Pursuing court action can be very time-consuming and stressful.

 Now try this

Scan this QR code to go the www. gov.uk website that will be of help.

How much is the court fee to make a claim for (a) £10,000 and (b) £100,000?

The doctrine of precedent in court hierarchy

Once a point of law has been decided in a case, that statement of the law must be applied in all future cases containing the same material facts.

What is precedent?

Precedent is the system whereby judges follow the decisions made in previous cases. Because of this, decisions made in cases set out much of English law, known as **stare decisis**.

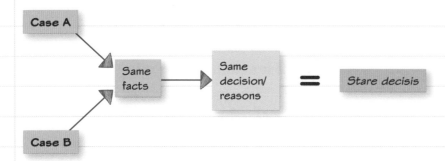

When a judge decides a case, they have to justify their decision. They do so by stating the relevant law and applying it to the facts of the case before the court.

This means that lawyers (and students of law) use decided cases to work out the law. The law can then be applied to the facts of a new case.

Precedent terms

These Latin terms have very specific meanings in English law.

Stare decisis – 'to stand by the decided decision'. It is based on the idea that if law is to be just and fair, it must be certain.

Ratio decidendi – 'the reason for deciding'. It means the rule of law on which the judge's decision is based and is set out in the judgment of a case.

Obiter dicta – 'words said as an aside'. These are part of the judge's opinion set out in the judgment but are not essential to the decision.

Precedent and court hierarchy

The decisions made by a court at one level must be adhered to by courts of the same or a lower level.

Precedents set in the Supreme Court and the Court of Appeal are **binding precedents** on courts of the same or lower level. However, in certain circumstances the Supreme Court may not abide by its previous decisions, and the Court of Appeal has the right to refuse to follow one of its previous decisions.

Precedent and the law of negligence

The law of negligence is nearly all based on precedents. Where there is an Act of Parliament, the meaning of that Act is interpreted by judges in cases. This sets a new precedent about the meaning of the Act of Parliament. These precedents are then applied in new cases.

What is a judgment?

A judgment includes the law on which the decision is based (the **ratio decidendi**) and may also include the judge's thoughts about whether the law should be interpreted differently or other points that are not directly relevant but should be considered (**obiter dicta**).

Think about which part of the judge's statement is essential to this case.

Now try this

In a decision, the judge makes the following statement in a case about an uncontrolled dog biting someone:

'It is clear from previous cases that all dogs must be controlled when on the street, for example, by being on a lead. I do not think this would apply to a cat or a rabbit.'

Explain which part of the statement is the *ratio decidendi* and which part is *obiter dicta*.

The hierarchy of the courts

There must be a defined court structure for precedent to work.

Court hierarchy

The general principle is that the decisions of a court at one level must be followed by all courts of the same or lower levels. However, there are sometimes exceptions.

 Refer back to page 2 for more on court hierarchy.

> The Supreme Court
> ▲
> The Court of Appeal
> ▲
> Courts of first instance

Changing names

The House of Lords was the previous name for the Supreme Court. The name was changed in 2009 to emphasise the difference between the House of Lords as one of the Houses of Parliament and the judicial House of Lords.

The House of Lords and the 1966 Practice Statement

Until 1966, the judicial House of Lords (now known as the Supreme Court) was bound by its previous decisions. The 1966 Practice Statement permitted the House of Lords to 'depart from its previous decisions'. In action, this meant that normally binding decisions could be disregarded 'when it appeared right to do so'.

In order to maintain certainty in law, the Supreme Court (pictured) very rarely uses the right, given by the 1966 Practice Statement, to depart from its previous decisions.

The Court of Appeal

The Court of Appeal must follow decisions made by the Supreme Court and its own previous decisions.

However, the case study opposite of **Young v Bristol Aeroplane Co** demonstrates that there are circumstances when the court can refuse to follow its own decisions.

Key term

Per incuriam is a Latin expression meaning without taking into account a relevant precedent or Act of Parliament. It literally means 'through lack of care'.

 Young v Bristol Aeroplane Co 1944

Scenario: This case involved compensation for a workman, under the Workmen's Compensation Acts.

Outcome: It set out three circumstances where the Court of Appeal could refuse to follow one of its own decisions.

- There are two conflicting decisions of the Court of Appeal.
- The decision of the Court of Appeal conflicts with a later Supreme Court decision.
- The Court of Appeal decision was decided *per incuriam*.

Now try this

Using the court hierarchy in the diagram above, explain which other courts' precedents must be followed by each court.

Ratio decidendi and obiter dicta

Not every statement the judge makes in a case can form a precedent. There are two parts to a decision.

Obiter dicta

This is the term used for all other things stated in a judgment that are not directly related to the decision.

Obiter dicta are known as persuasive precedents and do not have to be followed by a court of the same or lower level.

The effect of *obiter dicta*

Obiter dicta are often comments by a judge that might suggest where a change in the law is desirable but that they are unable to make because they are bound by a precedent of a higher court. Even the Supreme Court sometimes states that the law needs to change but suggests this is a job for Parliament.

Ratio decidendi

This is the legal reason for the decision and it forms a binding precedent.

The *ratio decidendi* of the decision is the binding element of the decision and must be followed by a court of the same or a lower level.

Lord Denning was perhaps the foremost judge of the 20th century. After qualifying as a barrister in 1923, he rose to become Master of the Rolls, the second most senior judge in England and Wales, before retiring in 1983.

Reading decisions

It is not always easy to distinguish *ratio decidendi* from *obiter dicta* when reading a decision. Law reports can be helpful in identifying *ratio* and *obiter* so lawyers can establish what law they should rely on and use, and which may persuade a court to decide in their favour.

Note that judges often abbreviate *obiter dicta* and *ratio decidendi* to 'obiter' and 'ratio'.

Lord Denning described the task of distinguishing between *ratio decidendi* and *obiter dicta* as 'formidable'.

 Key study   **Donoghue v Stevenson 1932**

Scenario: Mrs Donoghue went to have an ice cream float in a café. Part of the contents of a bottle of ginger beer made by Stevenson were in the float. Mrs Donoghue drank some of the float. When she poured out the rest of the ginger beer, she found a half-decomposed snail in the bottle. The bottle was opaque, so she could not have seen the snail. She claimed damages for shock and a stomach upset. The drink had been bought for her, so she had no contract with either the café or the manufacturer.

Outcome: Her claim was successful. This case established the modern law of negligence. The *ratio decidendi* was that manufacturers owe a duty of care to the ultimate consumers of their products.

Now try this

Access the appeal to the case **Darnley v Croydon Health Services NHS Trust 2017** via the QR code.

1   What key distinction was made by Lord Justice Jackson?

2   Is his decision about the receptionist *obiter dicta* or *ratio decidendi*?

3   What did Lord Justice McCombe say about a hospital having a duty not to misinform patients?

Other versions can be seen with an internet search but make sure the results refer to the 2017 appeal.

If you prefer a different case, you can look at other recent cases on websites such as the Temple Library site at the URL given in the link here.

Law reporting

A law report is a record of the judge's decision that sets a precedent.

Law reporting of decisions

Law reports are only published when the case:

- sets out a new principle of law
- makes a change to the law
- clarifies an aspect of the existing law.

Types of law report

Law reports are either full text law reports or summary reports.

- **Full text reports** include the full judgment of the court and a summary – or headnote – of the case.
- **Summary reports** may also be called case summaries, digests, case notes, etc. They are less formal and shorter than law reports and are a useful overview of the law but are not used to prove a precedent.

Layout of a law report

Here is an example of a headnote from Caparo v Dickman 1990. A headnote is a summary of a point of law that is included at the beginning of a law report to help the reader identify the discussion of a legal issue in an opinion.

The reference, so you can find the law report

The court, so you know if it is liable to be a binding precedent

The Law Reports (Appeal Cases)

[1990] 2 AC 605

[HOUSE OF LORDS]

The name of the case

CAPARO INDUSTRIES PLC. RESPONDENTS AND DICKMAN AND OTHERS APPELLANTS

Date when the case was heard

1989 Nov. 16, 20, 22, 23, 27, 28;

1990 Feb. 8

The judges who presided over the case

Lord Bridge of Harwich, Lord Roskill, Lord Ackner, Lord Oliver of Aylmerton and Lord Jauncey of Tullichettle

Negligence–Duty of care to whom?–Auditor–Appointment by company to audit and certify company's accounts–Statutory duty to make report to shareholders–Another company making take-over bid by initial purchase of shares–Claim that subsequent completion of take-over by purchase of total issued shares made in reliance on negligently made audit–Whether auditor owing duty of care to shareholders–Whether duty owed to non-shareholding investor–Companies Act 1985 (c.6), ss. 236(1)(2), 237(1)

The **facts** of the case are then summarised and the **decision** is set out following the word 'Held' (which means 'decided'), together with a list of other cases (precedents) referred to in the judgments.

Now try this

Find the full law report for **Caparo v Dickman 1990**. See the headnote and summary and then how much legal argument is made by the judges. Write a brief note explaining the structure of the law report.

Follow the BAILII link here:

Following precedent

There are two types of precedents: binding precedents and persuasive precedents.

 Links The powers of appeal courts to refuse to follow a precedent have been set out on page 18.

Binding precedent

The law set out in a binding precedent must be used in all courts unless the case is in the Supreme Court and the 1966 Practice Statement can be applied. Additionally, the case could be in the Court of Appeal and one of the conditions in **Young v Bristol Aeroplane Co 1944** can be used.

The essential point is that for a precedent to be binding on a judge in a later case, the material facts of the two cases must be similar.

Remember that material facts are the facts that are relevant to the court's decision.

 Links See page 19 to remind yourself of the Young v Bristol Aeroplane Co case.

Persuasive precedent

A persuasive precedent is one that is not a binding precedent but may be helpful to a court in making a decision. This could occur where a lower court makes a decision and a higher court decides to adopt the precedent in a similar case that has slightly different material facts.

Lawyers will bring up evidence to argue that the material facts of their case are effectively the same as a decision made in an inferior court.

The judge then must decide if the case is sufficiently similar to allow them to use the case in the current trial.

New areas of the law

Persuasive precedent is often argued where there are no similar cases, for example in a new area of law, such as virtual property, liability for driverless cars or drones, and IVF. In these areas, persuasive precedent may be the only precedent available.

The popularity of drones, particularly in urban areas, has prompted consideration of associated legal issues.

In the UK, the use of drones is regulated by the Civil Aviation Authority, who have developed a 'dronecode'.

Now try this

A (fictitious) case decided in the Court of Appeal states that a local authority does not owe a duty of care to road users over where they place road signs.

Mo was injured when he lost control of his bike and hit a lamp post.

1 Explain why the case is likely to prevent a successful claim for him against the local authority responsible for the lamp post.

2 If Mo did make a claim, at which level of appeal court might he have the possibility of a successful claim?

Consider examples of different levels of court, different material facts and new situations (such as where a drone is involved in the accident).

Avoiding binding precedents

A judge may wish to avoid having to follow a binding precedent because a precedent is outdated or a previous decision was made in error. They can do this in four ways.

Distinguishing   Overruling

Avoiding binding precedents

Reversing   Disapproving

Distinguishing and overruling

A binding precedent can be avoided if a judge can **distinguish** the current case from the precedent. They could do this by finding different material facts.

A precedent can be **overruled** if a court concludes that it is wrong and no longer demonstrates good law.

 Key study **Balfour v Balfour 1919 distinguished in Merritt v Merritt 1970**

Scenario: Distinguishing

Outcome: In **Balfour v Balfour**, the couple were living together when the agreement was made. This was distinguished in **Merritt v Merritt** as the couple were already separated when the agreement was made.

 Key study **Davis v Johnson 1979 overruled by Pepper v Hart 1993**

Scenario: Overruling

Outcome: In **Pepper v Hart**, the decision overruled the decision in **Davis v Johnson** which said that Hansard could not be consulted in trying to interpret an Act of Parliament.

Reversing and disapproving

Reversing occurs when a higher court changes the decision of a lower court on appeal against its decision.

Disapproving occurs where the court decides that the precedent is not relevant and goes on to make the point that the precedent should not be good law.

 Key study **Gillick v West Norfolk and Wisbech AHA 1986**

Scenario: Reversing

Outcome: The House of Lords (now the Supreme Court) reversed the decision of the Court of Appeal.

 Key study **R v Jordan 1956; R v Smith 1959**

Scenario: Disapproving

Outcome: Occurred with respect to the criminal cases of **R v Jordan 1956** which was disapproved in the case of **R v Smith 1959** with respect to medical treatment breaking the chain of causation.

Now try this

Research the cases of **Balfour v Balfour 1919** and **Merritt v Merritt 1970** and write down how the court in **Merritt** was able to distinguish **Balfour** and so not be bound by the precedent.

Researching and interpreting case law

This page considers how to research, find, read and interpret case law.

Case law

Precedent is the system whereby judges follow the decisions made in previous cases. You therefore need to be able to find relevant precedents for the situation you are researching. Remember that decided cases also interpret Acts of Parliament and so set precedents as to the meaning of Acts of Parliament and the Sections within them.

Researching case law

You can find relevant cases referred to in decided cases – most law reports will collect all case names referred to in judgments and list them.

Once you know a key case, many others will follow that are linked to it, either in textbooks or in articles in legal journals or on the internet.

You can also find linked cases on a number of websites, such as http://swarb.co.uk.

Reading a case

Start by reading the summary – does the case seem relevant to what you want to demonstrate? Examine other cases linked to the one you are looking at to see if any are more relevant.

To support your understanding, find the full law report.

Interpreting a case

Claimant   Defendant   Year of the case   Court is England and Wales Court of Appeal (EWCA)

Breakspeare v Pawlowski [2006] EWCA Civ 451

Civil division of the Court of Appeal   Page number in the law reports

View the full case on the BAILLI website:

The value of summaries

Law reports are often long and complex. Look for summaries and advice to clients. You may wish to consider this by looking for cases in articles aimed at clients of solicitors, or from barristers' chambers promoting their barristers.

Blogs

Some blogs are excellent – these are ones run by lawyers rather than student forums. So while the blog by Nigel Poole QC at the link here is fine, others written by non-experts should be avoided.

Be wary of tweets and other social media as a valid source of information.

Now try this

Find three reliable sources of case law on the internet. Try to do so for the case of **Darnley v Croydon NHS Trust 2017**. Note that you are looking for the decision in the Court of Appeal. Ignore any websites that you are unsure of and those that are not based in the UK.

Look for professional websites such as www.iclr.co.uk or http://swarb.co.uk. Do **not** use any non-UK websites!

Advantages and disadvantages of the doctrine of precedent

Making law and applying it is not always straightforward. Judges have the power through the system of judicial precedent to make new precedents.

Advantages of precedent

👍 The major advantage of precedent is that there is certainty – two cases with the same material facts will have the same outcome.

👍 This allows lawyers to advise their clients quickly and with precision.

👍 If there are not the same material facts, then there may be some flexibility so that a just outcome can be reached. There will still be a good indication of the outcome on the basis of similar cases with slightly different material facts.

Disadvantages of precedent

👎 The major disadvantage is the sheer volume of cases that contain precedents. Lawyers could be overwhelmed by this as it is not always easy to decide what the *ratio decidendi* of a decision is.

👎 When cases are distinguished, this can be very detailed, so a lot of work is required to unpick the law which can appear to have a level of uncertainty.

👎 If a decision seems questionable, there is no immediate way of changing this situation – it all depends on the level of appeal necessary. The rigidity of precedent means modifying the law can be time-consuming and expensive, particularly as specialists in the area of law will need to be consulted.

Certainty ─── Precision ─── **Advantages** ─── Flexibility ─── Time saving

Large number of cases ─── Finding the *ratio decidendi* in a case ─── **Disadvantages** ─── Uncertainty caused by distinguishing ─── Rigidity

Precedent can save a lawyer's time and their client's money.

Working through lots of case studies can be time-consuming for a lawyer and costly for their client.

Now try this

- In a negligence case, the court stated that where the defendant drove his car into the back of the car in front of him, he had been negligent.
- Another decided case states that a local authority can be negligent if they do not follow the requirements for gritting icy roads.
- A third case states that where a vehicle has spilled diesel on a wet road, it can be liable in negligence for an accident caused by this.

John drove around a corner and hit the car in front, which was reversing to go around a car that had crashed on an icy patch.

1 Outline the reasons why the cases might be precedent in John's case.

2 Explain why it would be different if the crash was on a motor racing circuit.

Duty of care: proximity

In cases of **negligence**, to decide whether a duty of care is owed by the defendant to the claimant, there is a three-part test. This page looks at the first part of the test, **proximity**.

Proximity

Proximity means closeness. Proximity between the claimant and the defendant is essential if a duty of care is to be owed. Proximity may arise because they are close in space and time when the event occurs or because of closeness of relationship to the person injured by the defendant.

Three-part test

The three parts of the test for duty of care set out in **Caparo v Dickman** are:

- Proximity
- Foreseeability
- Fair, just and reasonable.

 Links You can revise the other two parts on pages 27 and 28.

 Key study ## Bourhill v Young 1943

Scenario: The claimant was a pregnant woman. As she got off a tram, the defendant drove by on his motorcycle at excessive speed and crashed with a car 50 feet away from where the claimant was standing. The defendant was killed in the collision. The claimant heard the collision but did not see it. Later, the claimant walked past the accident scene where there was a lot of blood on the road. The claimant went into shock and subsequently labour, and her baby was stillborn. She brought a negligence claim against the defendant's estate.

Outcome: Mrs Bourhill was **unsuccessful** because she did not witness the accident, only heard it from a distant safe place. She then went to view the aftermath of the accident so was not present at the accident in time or space.

Bourhill v Young is a good precedent to use when considering proximity in **space and time**.

 Key study ## McLoughlin v O'Brian 1983

Scenario: The claimant's husband and three of her children were involved in a serious road accident when their car was hit by a lorry as a result of the negligence of the defendant lorry driver. One of the children died instantly. Another of the claimant's children was in a car behind the family. The driver took him home and told his mother of the incident, immediately driving her to the hospital. Here, she saw her family suffering before they had been treated. As a result, she suffered severe shock, organic depression and a personality change. She brought an action against the defendant for the psychiatric injury she suffered.

Outcome: Mrs McLoughlin was **successful** under the principle set out in **Bourhill v Young**. She was successful because she was the wife of one victim and the mother of another. She did not see the accident but as soon as she knew of the accident, she rushed to the hospital. This is a perfectly reasonable reaction given her proximity of relationship to the victims of the accident.

McLoughlin v O'Brian is a good precedent to use when considering proximity caused by **relationship**.

Now try this

Sal was sitting in her home when she heard a car crash in the street outside. She went outside to take photos of the accident on her phone. She left the scene and went back inside when the emergency services arrived. She then looked at her photos and realised one of the most severely injured victims was her cousin. She suffered shock as a result of the discovery.

Write down the arguments for and against sufficient proximity for that aspect of a duty of care. Reread your arguments and come to a reasoned conclusion.

 Remember, all three parts of the test in **Caparo v Dickman** must be proved for a duty of care to be owed. Consider this case again after you have revised **foreseeability** and the requirement that a duty must be **fair, just and reasonable** on pages 27 and 28.

Duty of care: foreseeability

To decide whether a duty of care is owed by the defendant to the claimant, there is a three-part test set out in **Caparo v Dickman**. This page looks at the second part of the test, **foreseeability**.

Foreseeability

This requires that the defendant's actions are ones that can be foreseen by the reasonable person to cause loss or damage to anyone in the claimant's position.

> **Links** For the other two parts of the three-part test, see pages 26 and 28.
> For more information on defining a reasonable person, see pages 29 and 30.

Three-part test

The three-part test set out in the case of **Caparo v Dickman** includes:

- proximity
- foreseeability
- fair, just and reasonable.

The reasonable person and foreseeability

The reasonable person has to see the injury or loss to someone in the claimant's position. It does not matter whether the defendant foresees this or not. Nor does the defendant have to foresee that the actual claimant would be injured or suffer loss as the test is whether a reasonable person in the defendant's position could foresee the loss. It is an objective test.

> The **defendant** is the party who causes the accident. The **claimant** is the party who has suffered injury or loss.

🔍 Key study Kent v Griffiths 2000

Scenario: Mrs Kent, an asthmatic, had waited approximately one and a half hours for an ambulance to arrive in response to a 999 call by her doctor. She suffered respiratory arrest before she got to hospital.

Outcome: The doctor gave evidence that had she known of the delay she would have advised the claimant's husband to drive her to the hospital. It is foreseeable to the reasonable person that anyone might be injured or suffer loss from an unreasonably delayed response to a 999 call for an ambulance.

Now try this

Naseem was driving behind a truck driven by Zak. As the truck rounded a bend, some fence posts in the truck fell out onto the road. Naseem could not avoid the posts, which damaged her car. The next day, Anthony, a cyclist, rode over some of the debris and got a puncture.

Explain whether damage to someone in Naseem's or Anthony's position is foreseeable to the reasonable person.

Duty of care: fair, just and reasonable

To decide whether a duty of care is owed by the defendant to the claimant, there is a three-part test set out in **Caparo v Dickman**. This page looks at the third part of the test: whether it is **fair, just and reasonable** to impose a duty of care on the defendant.

Why fair, just and reasonable?

Courts tend to be unwilling to make public bodies, such as the police, liable in negligence. This is seen as a matter of **public policy**. Public bodies should be able to decide how their resources should be best used and how to deal with their work without interference from the courts.

This will also prevent the **floodgates of litigation** opening.

Terms used in the principle

Public policy – the opinion that 'harm' to the public good is a reason for denying the existence of a duty of care.

Floodgates of litigation – a restraint to stop thousands of cases being brought against public bodies which could waste resources including time and money. This would eventually lead to poor service to the public because of monetary cuts and, for example, defensive policing to avoid claims.

Key study

Hill v Chief Constable of West Yorkshire 1988

Scenario: Peter Sutcliffe, the so called Yorkshire Ripper, had murdered several women in Yorkshire. The claimant's daughter was the killer's last victim before he was caught. By the time of her death the police already had enough information to arrest the killer, but had failed to do so. The mother claimed that the police owed a duty of care to her daughter.

Outcome: In this case it was not considered fair, just and reasonable to impose a duty of care.

Examples of public bodies

Besides the police, public bodies who work as part of the fire service have also been involved in duty of care cases. Other cases include:

- local authorities, as in **Mitchell v Glasgow City Council 2009**
- the police service, as in **Ancell v McDermott 1993**
- **Orange v Chief Constable of West Yorkshire 2002**.

Usually, fire and rescue services are protected from a claim in negligence as a matter of public policy. Liability is not fair, just and reasonable.

Look at page 24 to remind yourself how to research a case.

Now try this

Select one of the following cases. Find details of the case and write a short note about the case you have chosen to be shared with your class.

- **Michael v Chief Constable of South Wales 2015**
- **Sarjantson v Humberside Police 2013**
- **Tyrrell v Coroner for County Durham And Darlington 2016**
- **Rabone and Another v Pennine Care NHS Trust 2013**
- **Hertfordshire Police v Van Colle 2008**
- **Smith v Chief Constable of Sussex Police 2008**
- **Rathband v Chief Constable of Northumbria 2016**

The objective standard

This page explains the role of the objective standard in the law of negligence.

Objective and subjective standards

An **objective test** requires the court to view the circumstances from the standpoint of a hypothetical reasonable person and not the defendant. For example, one part of the test in **Caparo v Dickman** requires that the defendant's actions are ones that can be foreseen by the reasonable person to cause loss or damage to anyone in the claimant's position.

A **subjective test** requires the court to view the circumstances from the standpoint of the defendant.

> Objective test
> As seen by the reasonable person

> Subjective test
> As seen by the defendant

Negligence is objective

The idea that negligence is objective is explained in the famous quotation from Baron Alderson in **Blyth v Birmingham Waterworks 1856**:

> 'Negligence is the omission to do something, which a reasonable person,... would do, or doing something, which a prudent and reasonable person would not do.
>
> The standard demanded is thus not of perfection but of reasonableness. It is an objective standard taking no account of the defendant's incompetence – he may do the best he can and still be found negligent...'

Who is the reasonable person?

'... commuters on the London Underground ...'
Lord Steyn in 1999

'... the man on the Clapham omnibus ...'
Lord Justice Greer in 1933

 Key study **Dunnage v Randall 2015**

Scenario: The claimant had suffered burns when his uncle, who had unknowingly been suffering with a mental illness, had set fire to himself.

Outcome: The Court of Appeal said that no distinction should be drawn between physical and mental illness. So a defendant who was impaired by medical problems could not escape liability if he caused injury by failing to exercise reasonable care unless his condition was so serious that it entirely eliminated his responsibility.

 Links Look at page 27 for more on the reasonable person.

What the Court of Appeal stated about the objective test

The Court of Appeal made the following statement in the case of **Dunnage v Randall 2015**.

> 'The objective standard of care reflects the policy of the law. It is not a question of the law discriminating unfairly against people with physical or mental illness. The law takes the view as a matter of policy that everyone should owe the same duty of care for the protection of innocent victims.'

Now try this

Outline areas of law and cases that involve objective and subjective tests in tort law. Separate objective and subjective tests so you do not confuse them in your work.

The reasonable person test

People who are professionals, learners or not adults have a variation on the standard of care that is normally defined by the reasonable man (page 29). This page shows how the objective test is applied to those different types of defendant.

Special characteristics of defendants

The law considers three different types of defendant in terms of whether they are a reasonable person.

The categories are:

 professionals

 learners

 children (under 18 years old).

Defining a reasonable person

The reasonable person is the ordinary person doing things. Everyone should be the same when performing the same task. The standard is, therefore, judged against the reasonably competent person performing the task.

This means that victims are protected whoever has been performing the task.

If children are involved, they are usually judged by the standard of the child of the same age.

Professionals

It must be shown that the professional's conduct fell below the standard of a reasonably competent professional in the same area of expertise in order to prove a breach of duty of a professional.

> **Key study** **Bolam v Friern Hospital Management Committee 1957**
>
> **Scenario:** The claimant, Mr Bolam, underwent electric shock treatment at a mental health hospital. The doctor did not give him any relaxant drugs beforehand and the claimant suffered a serious fracture during treatment.
>
> **Outcome:** The duty had not been breached because the doctor reached the standard required by medical opinion, even though there were different medical opinions as to whether relaxant drugs should be given before this treatment.

② Learners

To prove breach of a duty of care of someone learning a skill or profession, they are compared with a reasonably competent person with that skill or of that profession.

> **Key study** **Nettleship v Weston 1971**
>
> **Scenario:** The defendant, Mrs Weston, was a learner driver who was being given lessons by a friend, the claimant, Mr Nettleship. He had checked that her insurance covered her for passengers before agreeing to go out with her. On one lesson, Mrs Weston mounted the pavement and hit a lamp post. Mr Nettleship fractured his knee.
>
> **Outcome:** The court decided that a learner driver is responsible and owes a duty of care to people in the car and on or near the highway.
>
> The standard of care expected of a learner driver is that of the reasonably competent driver.

---

③ Children

To prove breach of a duty of care by children, they are compared with an ordinary young person of the same age.

> **Key study** **Mullin v Richards 1998**
>
> **Scenario:** Mullin and Richards were school friends who were play fighting with plastic rulers. One of the rulers snapped and a fragment of plastic went into Mullin's eye, blinding her in that eye.
>
> **Outcome:** Richards was found not to be in breach of duty. She was only expected to meet the standard of a reasonable 15-year-old, not that of a reasonable adult.

Now try this

Examine the cases featured on this page and the decision the court arrived at. Explain why the court came to each decision.

Remember the important part is *why* the court came to the decision on the facts given.

Risk factors and breach of duty 1

When considering breach of duty, the law looks at the risks that a reasonable person can and should consider before they act.

Risk

- The reasonable person takes precautions against likely risks. If they do so, they will not have breached their duty of care.

- A reasonable person will take more care when they know there is a higher risk. If they do not do so, they are likely to have breached their duty of care.

- However, a reasonable person cannot take precautions against every eventuality.

> In the case of **Miller v Jackson**, the reasonable person would take more precautions and would breach their duty if the ball caused damage or injury to someone in the houses or gardens behind the ground.

Risk of harm

The risk factor, the risk of harm, is based on the general principle that the greater the risk, the more care must be taken if there is not to be a breach of duty. The greater the risk, the more care must be taken if there is not to be a breach of duty. However, if the risk is minimal, the reasonable person does not need to take precautions.

 Bolton v Stone 1951

Scenario: Miss Stone was injured when she was hit by a cricket ball while outside her home. The cricket field was surrounded by a 2-metre-high fence and the distance from the wicket was nearly 100 metres. A witness who lived close to the claimant said that during the last 30 years he had known balls hit his house or come into the yard five or six times. Two members of the cricket club agreed that the hit was exceptional compared to anything previously seen on that ground.

Outcome: There was no breach of duty. The likelihood of harm was low and the defendant, who had provided a useful service to the community, had taken all practical precautions in the circumstances.

 Miller v Jackson 1977

Scenario: A new development of homes was built in close proximity to an existing cricket ground. Mrs Miller, the claimant, bought one of the houses and brought an action against the cricket club when, in spite of a higher fence being erected, a number of balls were hit over the houses and some property was damaged. Mrs Miller complained that she was unable to use her garden while matches were in progress.

Outcome: As there were regular incidents of the ball leaving the ground and affecting the public, it was judged that adequate precautions had not been taken.

Special characteristics of the claimant

One risk factor is whether any special characteristics of the claimant are known to the defendant. For example, if the reasonable person knows someone has a disability or is of a young age, they take more care to avoid injury to them.

Key study Paris v Stepney Borough Council 1951

Scenario: As a result of a war injury, the claimant only had sight in one eye. During his employment as a mechanic, a splinter of metal went into his sighted eye causing him to become completely blind. His employer, the council, knew of his eyesight problems but had not provided safety goggles.

Outcome: There was a breach of duty. The employer should have provided goggles because the seriousness of harm to the claimant would have been greater than that experienced by workers with sight in both eyes.

> If you took a three-year-old child to the playground, would you stay with them or just let the child play on the equipment unaccompanied?

> Research the case in more detail using the techniques discussed on page 24.

 Now try this

Read through the Key studies above. Choose one and explain why the court came to that decision.

Risk factors and breach of duty 2

When considering breach of duty, the law looks at the risks which a reasonable person can and should consider before they act. As well as considering special characteristics and the risk of harm, the law also looks at the risk factors of social utility and the taking of precautions.

Social utility

The reasonable person, in an emergency situation, takes more risks than they ordinarily would because, in an emergency situation, normal precautions are minimised for the greater good.

Taking precautions

The reasonable person takes reasonable precautions but does not take excessive precautions.

🔍 Key study **Watt v Hertfordshire County Council 1954**

Scenario: A woman had been involved in a traffic accident (which happened a short distance from the fire station). She was trapped underneath a lorry. In order to release the woman, the fire service needed to use a heavy lorry jack. The normal vehicle for carrying the jack to the scene of the accident was not available. The claimant, a fireman, was ordered with other firemen to lift the jack onto the back of a truck and to hold it during the short journey. When the truck braked, the jack fell onto the claimant's leg leading to severe injuries.

Outcome: There was no breach of duty. The emergency of the situation and utility of the defendant's conduct in saving a life outweighed the need to take precautions.

🔍 Key study **Latimer v AEC 1953**

Scenario: The claimant, Mr Latimer, was injured after he had slipped on the defendant's factory floor. The floor had become slippery after the factory had flooded due to very heavy rain. The defendant tried to make the floor as safe as possible by mopping up and placing sawdust in the most used places. They had also put up warning signs. It was mooted at the trial that the company could have closed the factory but this was not deemed necessary as it would have led to great expense.

Outcome: There was no breach of duty and no duty to close the factory. The defendant only had to take reasonable precautions to minimise the risk and they had done so.

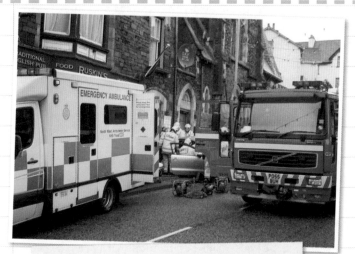

In the case of **Watt v Hertfordshire County Council**, Lord Denning said 'the saving of life or limb justifies taking considerable risk'.

The reasonable person takes precautions against likely risks, but they cannot take precautions against every eventuality such as the highly unusual circumstance of a vehicle driving into a building.

Now try this

Read through the Key studies above. Choose one and explain why the court came to that decision.

Research the case in more detail using the techniques discussed on page 24.

Factual causation

If a defendant has broken their duty of care, but this has not caused the loss which is being complained of, then the defendant is not liable for a claim in damages.

The 'but for' test

Factual causation is demonstrated through the 'but for' test. This test determines whether 'but for' the defendant's act or omission, the injury or loss would have occurred.

- If yes, the loss or omission would still have occurred, the defendant is not liable.
- If no, the loss or omission would not have occurred, the defendant is liable.

The Key study opposite demonstrates the 'but for' test in action.

 Barnett v Chelsea and Kensington Hospital Management Committee 1969

Scenario: Mr Barnett went to a hospital A&E department suffering from severe stomach pains and vomiting. He was not examined but advised by the duty doctor to go home and contact his GP. Mr Barnett died 5 hours later from arsenic poisoning.

Outcome: The hospital was not held liable as the doctor's failure to examine Mr Barnett did not lead to his death. Even if he had been examined, it was already too late to save his life.

Intervening acts

There is no factual causation where there is an intervening event that becomes the factual causation in an incident. The intervening act breaks the chain of causation.

Key study Knightley v Johns 1982

Scenario: The defendant, Mr Johns, overturned his car in a tunnel after driving negligently. The senior police officer at the scene forgot to close the tunnel so he ordered PC Knightley to ride back through the tunnel on his motorbike to close it. As he did so, PC Knightley was involved in another accident and was seriously injured.

Outcome: The second accident broke the chain of causation, as it was a new act intervening, so Mr Johns was not held liable for the injuries to PC Knightley.

Key legal principle – there is no liability in negligence if there is no factual causation.

 Apply the 'but for' test and consider whether there is an intervening act.

Now try this

Mohammed suffered a broken leg at work. This was agreed to be a result of negligence by his employer. He was being taken by ambulance to the hospital when a lorry driver crashed into the back of the ambulance. Mohammed suffered many other injuries because of the crash.

Is Mohammed's employer the factual cause of the broken leg and the other injuries in the crash? Explain your answer.

Remoteness of damage

If factual causation is proved, the defendant may still not be liable for a claim in damages if the damage is too remote from the original negligent act.

Reasonable foreseeability

The main test for remoteness of damage is that the damage must be reasonably foreseeable. This is an objective test: what losses (damage) could the reasonable person in the defendant's position foresee?

The type of damage caused

As long as the type of damage is foreseeable, the actual form of that type of damage can be extreme as seen in the case of **Bradford v Robinson Rentals 1967**.

 Reasonable foreseeability is an objective test you can add to the list you started on page 29.

 The Wagon Mound 1961

Scenario: The defendant's vessel, *The Wagon Mound*, leaked oil at a wharf in Sydney Harbour. Cotton debris became mixed with the oil, which was ignited by sparks from some welding works. The fire spread rapidly, destroying some boats and the wharf.

Outcome: In this case, although damage done to the wharf by oil being spilled was reasonably foreseeable, fire damage was not reasonably foreseeable and therefore was too remote to give rise to liability. In other words, the reasonable person could foresee damage from an oil spill, but not damage by fire.

 Bradford v Robinson Rentals 1967

Scenario: The claimant was sent by his employer to drive a long distance to exchange an old van for a new one during extremely cold weather conditions. Neither of the vehicles were heated and the window of one of them was stuck open. As a result, the claimant suffered frostbite.

Outcome: Although frostbite is rare, injury through cold exposure could be foreseen. Frostbite is just an extreme form of injury from being cold.

The thin skull rule

The 'thin skull' rule assumes that everyone and everything is different in a case.

Unknown to science

Damage is not reasonably foreseeable if the accident occurs as a result of an unknown type of event, as in the key study below.

 Smith v Leech Brain 1962

Scenario: As a result of his employer's negligence, Smith was burned on the lip by a splash of molten metal while at work. He had an existing pre-cancerous condition and the burn eventually brought about the onset of full cancer and Smith died.

Outcome: The company was liable to compensate for his death, as they had to take Smith as they found him, that is, with the pre-cancerous condition.

 Doughty v Turner 1964

Scenario: The cover on a cauldron of an exceedingly hot molten liquid was accidentally knocked into the cauldron. Doughty was injured when, a short time later, the cauldron erupted violently.

Outcome: Scientific knowledge at the time was that there might be a small splash, not a violent explosion, so the damage to Mr Doughty was too remote.

Now try this

In the case of **Hughes v Lord Advocate 1963**, a manhole had been left open and covered by a tent and a paraffin lamp. A child climbed down the hole. When he came out he knocked over one of the lamps which fell into the hole and caused an explosion. The child suffered burns.

Apply the principle in **Bradford v Robinson Rentals** to the **Hughes v Lord Advocate 1963** case. Explain whether the burns were too remote a consequence to make those who had left the manhole open liable.

Awarding damages and mitigating loss

If a defendant has broken their duty of care, and it has caused loss, they will be liable for a claim in damages. Damages are money that the defendant must pay to the claimant as compensation for the loss or injuries they have suffered.

Aim of damages

Damages are for the value of any goods destroyed or for their repair to return them to the condition they were in before the incident.

The general aim of damages in negligence is to put the successful claimant in the same position as they would have been in if the negligence had not occurred.

Distinctions

Damage is a legal concept which is the loss or injury suffered as a result of a breach of duty.

Damages is the amount of money that is awarded to compensate the victim for their loss or injury.

Damages

Damages can be divided into **special** and **general** damages.

Special damages are losses that can be calculated at the time of the trial, for example:

- repair of car or value of car immediately before an accident if it has been written off
- loss of earnings up to the date of the trial
- any expenses that have been incurred as a result of an accident.

General damages are all other forms of financial compensation, for example:

- loss of future earnings
- pain and suffering
- loss of amenity (ability to do things)
- future medical expenses.

 General damages and special damages are explored in more depth on page 36.

Mitigation of loss

The claimant is required to take reasonable action to keep their losses to a minimum and defendants cannot be forced to pay for avoidable losses. This means you must keep your losses to a minimum and follow the original aim of compensating you so far as possible to put you in the position you were in before the negligence. For example, if your kitchen has been damaged, it might not be reasonable to eat in a 5-star restaurant every day until your kitchen appliances have been replaced.

Keeping it fair

If your car is badly damaged and cannot be driven, hiring an expensive car is not reasonable if you have another car or if the car repairer has a courtesy vehicle available.

If you are self-employed doing limousine trips to airports and cannot work for some weeks, it is probably more cost effective to hire another driver for those few weeks rather than lose the business and goodwill of regular customers. Getting the alternative driver would be an example of you mitigating your loss.

Now try this

Explain whether the following damage resulting from the defendant's negligence are special or general damages:

1. An injury meaning the claimant cannot continue as a professional tennis player
2. Clothes ruined in an accident
3. Physiotherapist's fees to help rehabilitate the claimant
4. Wages lost before the trial of a claim
5. Future loss of earnings.

 It might help to draw up a table when you answer the question with three columns headed 'question'; 'special or general'; 'explanation'.

Damages

Remember that 'damages' means money that the defendant must pay, if they are found liable, to the claimant as compensation for the loss or injuries they have suffered. Damages can be 'special' – pecuniary – or 'general', including compensation for pain and suffering, loss of earnings, loss of amenity and future medical expenses.

Special damages: pecuniary

Pecuniary means monetary. This relates to damages awarded for financial losses such as damage to goods and lost earnings, and also any expenses incurred as a result of an accident, such as those relating to travel.

Non-pecuniary damages relate to non-financial ones, such as injuries. Remember: non-pecuniary damages are part of general damages as they cannot be easily quantified.

Pain and suffering

Calculating pain and suffering is challenging as every case is different. The amount will vary with the individual but will take into account medical reports. This, and loss of amenity, often use calculations based on awards in previous cases.

Lawyers also look at the Judicial College's (formerly Judicial Studies Board) Guidelines as they give an indication of the likely amount to be awarded.

Loss of earnings

Special damages for loss of earnings up to trial are relatively easy to calculate. Future losses are more difficult to calculate as they can only be estimated. However, the calculations used are designed to reflect an appropriate amount.

If you were a professional football coach, and you lost both your legs in a car accident that was not your fault, you could claim damages for loss of future earnings.

Loss of amenity

This term is the legal term used to describe the impact of the injury on the claimant's enjoyment of life. It can cover compensation for being confined in hospital and/or being left with a disability that stops you from doing things you could do before the injury occurred.

Future medical expenses

Again, this is an estimate based on cases where people have sustained similar injuries. Some injuries are such that the claimant requires professional nursing care and future medical treatment.

Heads of damage

The expression 'heads of damage' is used to describe the constituent parts of a claim for damages. This means what the amount of damages is made up of.

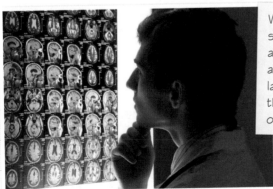

Where there is a severe brain injury, the amount of damages awarded may be very large, reflecting both the level and intensity of care required.

Guidelines for the level of damages awarded for specific injuries, and levels of injury, are available at the link here: www.rcsolicitors.co.uk.

Now try this

Review the Judicial College's Guidelines for the assessment of general damages on the internet. Select three different types of injury and explain their typical awards.

Contributory negligence

Contributory negligence occurs when the claimant is found to be partly responsible for the damage they suffered.

The principle

If a claimant has contributed to the losses they have suffered, then a proportion of the damages will be lost. The amount lost depends on the degree to which the claimant's own acts are negligent. The reduction can be between 0% and 100%.

The Law Reform (Contributory Negligence) Act 1945

This Act of Parliament sets out the law. The court can reduce damages:

'to such extent as the court thinks just and equitable having regard to the claimant's share in the responsibility for the damage.'

In practice

In a theoretical example where the claimant was to be awarded £1000 damages, but was found to be 10% contributorily negligent, they would actually receive £900.

The 10% reduction has been taken off the £1000.

Their £900 is then seen as the true value of their claim, bearing in mind the claimant's fault with respect to the accident.

 Key study **Sayers v Harlow Council 1958**

Scenario: Mrs Sayers was found to be partly the author of her own downfall when she attempted to climb out of a toilet cubicle; the door lock had failed, locking her in. She stepped first on to the toilet and then on to the toilet-roll holder, which gave way, causing her to fall and sustain injuries.

Outcome: The court reduced the damages by 25% since she had been contributorily negligent in the way in which she tried to escape from the locked cubicle.

Automatic contributory negligence

There are a number of examples where contributory negligence is seen automatically. One of them is the failure to wear a seatbelt in a vehicle fitted with one.

However, the court still takes into account whether the seatbelt would have:

1 prevented injury, or

2 reduced the severity of the injury, or

3 made no difference to the injury.

Typically the three circumstances above would result in a 25% reduction, a 15% reduction and no reduction in the damages awarded.

 Now try this

 Many lawyers specialise in personal injury cases. Find a website and select two examples where there may have been contributory negligence.

 Make brief notes to explain the facts of the case and the outcome.

Try searching on the internet for the case of **Smith v Finch [2009] EWHC 53 (QB)**, for example.

 Search for 'contributory negligence' at www.farrarsbuilding.co.uk/.

How damages are paid

Damages are usually paid as a lump sum. However, some larger awards are paid through a structured settlement.

Payment of damages

Damages are compensation and therefore need to be paid in such a way that the claimant is not advantaged or disadvantaged. For example, a claimant is potentially advantaged if a very large sum is paid up front to cover future needs, but those needs never occur because the claimant dies shortly after they receive the sum. This would not reflect the costs and losses to the claimant as a result of the accident and could encourage some to hasten the death of the claimant in order to inherit the money.

Lump sums

A lump sum means that the damages are paid all at once. In most cases, this is not problematic as most claims are settled by insurance companies. However, if not paid through an insurer, the claimant may have difficulty getting the payment from the defendant.

Special damages are always paid by a lump sum.

Structured settlements

In large personal injury and medical negligence claims, a structured settlement is an alternative to receiving a lump sum.

A structured settlement may include:

- interim payments – to cover expenses already made
- regular instalments – usually paid through an **annuity** so there is a regular income throughout the injured person's life
- a further lump sum payment to cover extra costs that are not covered by the annuity payment.

Why a structured settlement?

A structured settlement may be used so that:

 the injured person does not have to manage a large sum of money

 there is less chance of the claimant 'blowing' the money and becoming destitute

 there is less risk of running out of money for care

 the claimant will get compensation and not more than they need

 life expectancy is not an exact science so finances are certain for the future

 family and friends cannot exploit the injured person and do not 'get a bonus' on the death of a claimant.

🔍 Key study   Walton v Calderdale NHS Trust 2005

Scenario: The claimant, born in July 1995, suffered from cerebral palsy as a result of being deprived of oxygen during birth. Liability for negligence was admitted and the case revolved around the amount of payments to be made. The claimant was severely handicapped and required a large level of care and assistance in most aspects of daily living. He had greatly reduced ability to communicate. However, his intellectual capacity and life expectancy were largely unaffected.

Outcome: The Trust paid the claimant – who had a life expectancy of 70 years when the settlement of the case was reached – an annual payment of £50,548, index linked, in respect of his annual care costs, rather than a lump sum.

Now try this

Using the facts of **Walton v Calderdale NHS Trust**, above, suggest two reasons why a lump sum was not appropriate in the case.

 Research the case further on the internet.

The burden of proof and res ipsa loquitur

The burden of proof explains who has to prove their case in a negligence claim – either the claimant or the defendant.

The burden of proof

The claimant must prove their case on a balance of probabilities.

This standard means that the court must be satisfied that the event in question is more likely to have occurred than not.

However, the burden of proof moves to the defendant if **res ipsa loquitur** applies.

Key term

Res ipsa loquitur is a Latin expression meaning 'the thing speaks for itself'.

The principle has been developed for situations where negligence can only be inferred from what happened and the exact cause cannot be proved by the claimant. Typically, this is because the injured person was unconscious at the time of, or as a result of, the incident.

Testing for res ipsa loquitur

The test to see if res ipsa loquitur applies requires three things to be proved by the claimant:

1 The thing that caused the damage was under the sole control of the defendant.

2 The incident is one that would not have happened unless someone had been negligent.

3 There is no other obvious reason as to why the incident occurred.

The effect

The burden of proof shifts from the claimant to the defendant if the principle of res ipsa loquitur applies. This means that the defendant would have to show they were not negligent by explaining how the incident happened.

 Scott v London & St. Katherine Docks Co 1865

Scenario: A customs officer was passing a warehouse and six sacks of sugar fell onto him from a crane operated by the warehouse.

Outcome: The defendant was held liable as res ipsa loquitur was found to apply:

1 The crane and sacks of sugar were under the sole control of the warehouse.

2 Sacks of sugar do not fall from cranes unless someone has been negligent.

3 How else could this have happened? There was no other obvious reason as to why the incident occurred.

Apply each of the three rules for res ipsa loquitur set out above.

 Now try this

 Mahon v Osborne 1939

Scenario: The claimant died following a routine surgical operation. A post mortem established that the cause of death was peritonitis as a result of a surgical swab being left inside his body when he was stitched up following the operation.

Outcome: Res ipsa loquitur applied.

Explain why res ipsa loquitur applied in this case.

Your Unit 1 set task

Unit 1 will be assessed through a task, which will be set by Pearson. In this assessed task, you will need to research the law of negligence. You will then be assessed on your ability to explain, analyse and apply to a scenario the law of negligence that you have researched.

Your assessed task could cover any of the essential content in the unit. You can revise the unit content in this Revision Guide. In this skills section, you can review extracts from responses to tasks similar to those you may be given as part of your assessment. This will help you to revise the essential skills you will need for your assessed task.

Outlining and applying – responding to stimulus material
Practise this skill on page 42.

Explaining and analysing – responding to stimulus material
Practise this skill on page 43.

Research and making notes
Revise research and note-making skills on page 41.

Evaluating – responding to stimulus material
Practise evaluating skills on page 44.

Set task skills

Case file notes
Practise skills for writing these notes on page 47.

Solicitors' letters
Revise skills for letter writing on page 46.

Making presentation slides
Practise your presentation skills on page 45.

Workflow

The process of preparing for your assessment should help you to explain, analyse and apply the law of negligence to a scenario, and might follow these steps:

- ✓ Read about cases involving the main aspects of negligence, including establishing a duty of care, what amounts to a breach of duty, and what loss or damage amounts to.
- ✓ Research aspects of law relating to duty, breach and damage.
- ✓ Make notes that will be useful in your assessment. Refer to the Pearson website for guidance on what notes you can take into your assessment.
- ✓ Read any further information provided about a particular scenario involving current law relating to negligence.
- ✓ Produce documents for members of the legal profession or for clients in relation to the current law relating to negligence for a particular scenario.

Check the Pearson website

This section is designed to demonstrate the skills that will be needed in your assessed task. The details of your actual assessed task may change from year to year so always make sure you are up to date. Check the Pearson website for the most up-to-date **Sample Assessment Material** and **Mark Scheme** to get an idea of the structure of your assessed task and what this requires of you.

Now try this

Visit the Pearson website and find the page containing the course materials for BTEC National Applied Law. Download the latest Unit 1 Sample Assessment Materials and make a note of:

- the structure of your set task, and whether it is divided into separate parts
- how much time you are allowed for each section of the task
- what briefing or stimulus material may be provided to you
- any notes you might have to make and whether you are allowed to take selected notes into your supervised assessment
- the activities you are required to complete and how to format your responses.

Research and making notes

As part of your assessment you will be asked to produce certain documents. You may be given some time to prepare for this in advance by carrying out some research on a particular area of law relating to negligence. As a starting point for your research, you may be provided with a case or relevant case law to review.

Apply the three-stage test to Joshua's case.

Consider who the case is against – the player or the team.

You have been given the file of a client Joshua Adam. Joshua was professional rugby player until he sustained life-changing injuries during a game. Joshua believes he has a case for negligence against his opponent who caused his injury.

What is the risk of harm? Were reasonable precautions taken?

Research notes

During your research, it would be helpful to write clear notes that you can use to help you later on.

- DO use bullet points.
- DO make sure your notes are relevant – they should relate to the scenario you have been given.
- DO refine the information that will be most helpful, for example, key facts and legal principles.
- DON'T write pages and pages – the amount of notes you can use in supervised assessment may be limited.
- DON'T copy large chunks of information – you won't be able to pick out the key points.

Preparatory notes

You may be allowed to take some of your preparatory notes into your supervised assessment time. If so, there may be restrictions on the content, length and type of notes that are allowed.

Check with your tutor or look at the most up-to-date Sample Assessment Material on the Pearson website for information.

Sample notes extract

Case notes

- **Caparo v Dickman 1990** – 3-stage test for showing duty of care – proximity of relationship, foreseeability of harm, it is fair just and reasonable to impose a duty of care.

- **Bolton v Stone 1951** – woman injured when cricket ball hit out of ground – the greater the possibility of harm, the more precautions should be taken. Claim failed as all appropriate precautions taken.

- **Barnett v Chelsea & Kensington Hospital 1969** – worker suffered stomach pains and was turned away from A&E. Later died from arsenic poisoning. Hospital not liable as he would have died anyway. D has to have caused injury or loss to C.

Note-taking can be in shorthand. For example, DofC for 'duty of care', C for Claimant, D for Defendant.

It will be less useful for you to write lots of facts about a case. The important thing is the point established by the case – the legal principle.

The task may require you to advise a client or other members of the legal profession. Think about the reader and the relevant terminology to use.

Ensure the cases you write notes on are relevant to the area of the law that may have been specified for you.

Now try this

Research another case relating to duty of care, such as **Hill v Chief Constable of West Yorkshire 1988**, and make notes on it using the tips given above.

Outlining and applying

You may need to use the skills of outlining or applying as part of the externally assessed task you are set. It is likely that you will be given a new scenario to which you will need to apply the information you have previously researched. Below is an example of a new case, and how previous research could be applied.

> Clara was cycling along her local high street when she was hit by an advertising board being installed on a nearby building. She was knocked unconscious and suffered several broken bones. Clara was unable to work for several weeks and she has been advised that she has a claim.

This is a civil tort case between Clara and the installers of the advertising board. It will be a claim of negligence which has caused personal injury, damage and loss to Clara. Think about what has to be proved in a negligence claim and what can be claimed by Clara if she is successful.

In your assessment, you may be asked to 'outline' which requires you to give a summary, overview or a brief description of an aspect of law or procedure.

You may also be asked to 'apply' your knowledge, which requires you to apply the law to the facts of a scenario and to reach a decision about a possible result.

In this extract from a letter – to the person who caused the accident – the writer has **outlined** clearly the basis of their client's case and claim.

Sample response extract

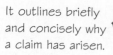 It outlines briefly and concisely why a claim has arisen.

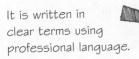 It is written in clear terms using professional language.

> As a result of your negligence, our client has suffered injury, damage to her bicycle and loss of earnings. We have advised her to make a claim against you for her losses and unless we hear from you within seven days accepting responsibility for the accident we intend to issue a court claim for damages.

It sets out what they want the recipient to do.

The consequences of not replying within a given time limit are clearly given.

This is an extract from a note for legal office files **applying** the rules on damages to Clara's case.

Sample response extract

The law is clearly applied by stating the purpose of the award of damages in tort and what can be claimed.

> I advised Clara that the purpose of the award of damages in tort is to put her back in the position she was in before the accident. As a result, she should be able to claim for the damage to her bicycle, and her loss or earnings as these directly resulted from the other driver's negligence. I asked her to get a written estimate for repairs to the bike and a letter from her employer confirming the amount of her loss of earnings.
>
> I advised Clara that she will have to have a medical report to assess the severity of her injuries and the firm would be contacting a specialist to arrange this.

The outcome Clara should expect is well defined and clearly presented.

This is a good answer as any reader of the note will be able to clearly see what advice Clara has been given and the purpose of the award of damages.

The writer also sets out what the next steps in the case should be – collecting relevant evidence.

Now try this

Clara has now been awarded damages. You have been asked to write to her outlining the two ways in which damages could be paid. Plan the structure and content of your letter.

Explaining and analysing

You may need to provide an explanation or an analysis as part of the externally assessed task you are set.

Explaining requires you to give clear details of an area of law or procedure and to give reasons and/or evidence to support an opinion, view or argument.

Analysing requires you to present the outcome of methodical and detailed examination of relevant law and procedure to the facts of a scenario and to reach a decision about a possible result.

This is an extract from a letter to a client in which the writer has been asked to **explain** the types of damages that can be claimed following a car accident.

Before you start writing, make a note of the points you want to cover and then see if they can be linked together.

Sample response extract

There are two forms of damages that can be claimed. Special damages cover specific amounts that have been lost or damaged. This can be damage caused to your car or lost wages while you were in hospital. General damages cover unspecified matters such as the pain and suffering you endured after the accident, any future medical expenses that you might have to pay and 'loss of amenity' to compensate you as you may not be able to play tennis in the future.

 The points are presented in a logical order.

 The learner writes in clear terms using professional language.

 This response clearly explains the two main types of damages that can be claimed with relevant examples of the type of losses that may apply.

In this extract, the writer has **analysed** the relevant law in a case file note.

The learner has used their research and notes (see page 41) about the principles of showing a duty of care to show that all three elements of a duty are satisfied.

Sample response extract

Both road users were in proximity to each other on the road. It is foreseeable that if one road user is careless then other road users may be injured. It is fair, just and reasonable that a careless road user should be legally responsible to others. In this case a duty of care can be shown as both our client and the defendant were road users at the time of the accident and it is well known that one road user owes another a duty of care. This duty has been broken as the defendant has driven carelessly by exceeding the speed limit meaning that there is a high risk of someone being injured. This excessive speeding led directly to the accident as our client had no opportunity to get out of the road in time to avoid being hit.

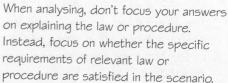

When analysing, don't focus your answers on explaining the law or procedure. Instead, focus on whether the specific requirements of relevant law or procedure are satisfied in the scenario.

 This is a good answer as it covers each of the three requirements of negligence in a logical order, justifying each in turn.

Now try this

Using the case of **Wells v Cooper 1958**, explain how this is an example of the reasonable person test in a file note.

Evaluating

You may need to provide an evaluation as part of the externally assessed task you are set.

Evaluating involves considering strengths and weaknesses of a case or identifying any advantages and disadvantages and looking at alternatives. You will need to form a judgement based on the points you have raised and this will usually be in the form of a conclusion.

Sample response extract

Using the civil courts is the traditional way of resolving a dispute as a final decision will be reached by a legally qualified judge after hearing all the evidence from both sides. Usually the result of the case can be predicted as judges have to use precedents from previous cases.

However, it may not be the best way of dealing with a dispute. Courts are expensive to use as it is likely that lawyers will represent both sides. These lawyers cost money and there is no guarantee that even what is thought to be a strong case will be won. Also, the loser of the case will have to pay the winner's costs as well as any compensation.

There are some alternatives that may be quicker, cheaper and less confrontational as there is less need for lawyers to be involved. These alternatives include negotiation, mediation or possibly arbitration. For some claimants they may be an attractive alternative to deal with a claim more speedily and cheaply.

However, it has to be remembered that if a case is taken without using legal advice the claimant may not receive as much compensation as they would be awarded using the courts and the case cannot be heard a second time. The result cannot always be predicted as precedent is not often used.

The alternatives to traditional courts provide useful options for dispute resolution in certain cases but they are not necessarily suitable in every case.

 This is an extract from a presentation in which the speaker has been asked to provide an evaluation of the routes of dispute resolution.

 The first two paragraphs summarise the advantages and disadvantages of using court-based resolution.

 Facts are clearly presented.

 Opinions are well laid out and supported by examples.

 The third and fourth paragraphs summarise the advantages and disadvantages of using alternative dispute resolution methods.

 Alternative ways of solving disputes are clearly explained.

 Opinions are well laid out and supported by examples.

 The final paragraph concludes with an overall summary.

Now try this

Using the case example of **Paris v Stepney B.C. 1951**, plan your evaluation of the likelihood of success for Mr Paris, the injured claimant, with a justified conclusion.

Presentations

In your external assessment, you may be required to prepare a presentation, perhaps to others in the firm, about a specific claim. This is likely to involve explaining relevant law and procedure and explaining how it could apply to the claim. You may also need to use your skills to outline, analyse or evaluate.

This page provides a format that you could use. It is always a good idea to plan your slides before writing them in full. You should create your slides, with notes if relevant, using presentation software such as PowerPoint.

Background to the case
Identify what the claim is about and what you will be covering during the presentation.

Set out the relevant law
In a negligence claim, this will be proof of duty of care, breach of duty and resulting loss or damage.

Explain where the relevant law can be found
Use precedent cases for each of duty, breach and damage.

Presentations

Summary and conclusion
Evaluate, considering everything covered in the presentation, if there is a claim and whether it is worth pursuing.

Apply the law and procedure to the case
Are all the requirements of negligence present? What precedent cases are relevant? How much is the claim likely to be worth? Which court will be used if no settlement is possible?

Explain any procedural issues
Outline which courts to use, amount of claim, obtaining of reports, how the claim could be funded, purpose of claim – obtaining damages, likelihood of settlement or using ADR.

Below is an extract (the first slide) from an example presentation covering the case of **Mullin v Richards 1998**.

Sample response extract

Slide 1 sets the scene and identifies the points you are going to deal with in the presentation.

Slides 2–5 will outline the case and the key points for review and consideration.

Slide 6 may cover whether there is proof of negligence, which court to issue a claim in, whether there are worthwhile alternatives such as ADR and next steps.

Client: Mullin
Case: Two schoolgirls were play fighting with plastic rulers. One of the rulers snapped and a piece of plastic hit Mullin in the eye causing her serious injury.
Relevant law: Negligence. What is the standard of care at which the girls should be judged?

Planning

☑ Organise the slides in a logical sequence – explain the law before applying it to the facts of a case.

☑ Avoid large blocks of text.

☑ Use bullet points or numbers for key issues.

☑ Have a maximum of six or seven points per slide.

☑ Use simple graphics or diagrams.

☑ Finish with a question for the audience to encourage discussion.

Now try this

Prepare slide 2 of the presentation for the example case of **Mullin v Richards 1998**.

Consider the requirements of breach of duty in negligence, the reasonable person test, how professionals and learners are judged and how children should be judged.

Writing solicitors' letters

In your external assessment, you may be required to write a professional letter, to someone who either does or does not have legal training. You may need to apply your legal knowledge and outline, analyse, explain or evaluate. It is a good idea to plan what you need to say, and use your communication skills to produce accurate, clear and concise information that is appropriate for the recipient.

Be accurate and outline key points clearly and concisely.

Use appropriate language, including professional legal terminology as appropriate, or clearly explaining terminology if the recipient has no knowledge of the law.

Use the appropriate format.

Solicitors' letters

Be relevant to the area of law and/or procedure involved.

Clearly outline the next steps and what is required.

Be polite.

Ensure that there are no spelling and grammatical errors.

Links Revise the content of a solicitor's letter on page 10.

Format and features of a solicitors' letter

You don't need to include a phone number or email address, just your firm's address. If you have been given the name of the firm but not the address, make one up.

The recipient's name and address (who you are writing to) is placed at the top left of the letter. This may be an individual (perhaps your client) or another firm (perhaps another legal firm).

Always include a date. If you have not been given a date, use the current date.

Include the subject of the letter in bold or underlined on a line of its own at the start.

Sign off using 'Yours sincerely' (if you used your client's surname) or 'Yours faithfully' (if you used 'Dear Sirs').

> Hawks and Lewis Solicitors
> 1 Stag Road
> Hertford
> HT1 1SL
>
> Mr G Brooks
> 8 Green Street
> Stafford
> ST8 8BD
>
> 15 May 2018
>
> Dear Mr Brooks
> **Ref. Accident claim**
> We write pursuant to the...
>
> Yours sincerely
>
> *A. Agnew*
>
> Alison Agnew

When writing to your client always use their surname prefixed with 'Dear' and a title such as 'Mr' or 'Ms'. Use 'Dear Sirs' if you are writing to another firm.

In the text of the letter use short, clear paragraphs. Do not use slang or 'text speak'. If you are writing to a client explain any legal words or procedures.

Include your name typed below your signature if writing a letter to your client, or the name of your firm if a letter to another legal firm.

Don't forget to proofread for spelling and grammar errors.

Now try this

Using your own example of a case (such as **Orchard v Lee 2009**), plan a short letter to your client asking what happened in the accident. Plan each paragraph of the letter, the format and layout, how it will start and its logical order. You should also identify the correct terminology, form of address and sign-off.

Case file notes

In your external assessment, you may be required to write notes for a client's file, perhaps to record what has been said in an interview or court hearing, for example, or to advise others in the firm of the law or procedure that should apply to the case in the future. You may need to use your skills to explain, outline, analyse or evaluate.

This page provides guidance on a format which you could use. It's always a good idea to plan the structure of a file note before you write it in full.

Give a detailed insight into the case, relevant law and the future of the case.

Provide full details of the client and their background.

Explain the facts of the case, how the accident happened and who was at fault.

Outline what is currently being actioned.

Provide clear instructions for what work others in the firm are required to do and when.

Case file notes

Outline the area of law involved and evaluate whether all requirements to prove the case are satisfied.

Detail what reports are required or outstanding – medical reports, witness reports, and so on.

Sample response extract

In this case file note extract the writer has outlined their client's case.

Client: Mr Arthur Hunt

Address: 25 Common Road, Headington, Oxford, OX1 3HY

D.O.B: 31 August 1956

Profession: Musician

Date of accident: 31 July 2017

Provide clear client details so they can be easily contacted.

We have been consulted by Mr Hunt who was riding his bicycle on a road through Morton Park when he collided with a dog, sustaining injury. Mr Hunt wants to pursue a claim for compensation. He has the name of the dog owner, Lydia Grant, who denied that her dog was at fault but we are yet to find if there were witnesses. Following the accident our client was taken to hospital by ambulance and after X-rays it was confirmed he had suffered a fractured right collarbone, a fractured right wrist, bruising and grazing to his right leg. A full medical report has been requested. He has been told he will be unable to work for up to 4 months. I advised that he has a possible claim for negligence and if proved he could expect to claim damages.

Next steps: Draft a claim for negligence.

Reference of who the case would be brought against.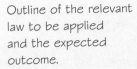

Outline of the relevant law to be applied and the expected outcome.

Specific instructions on what to do next should be provided.

Provide any details of any witnesses to help support Mr Hunt's claim.

Provide a clear overview of the extent of injuries so there can be a judgement on the seriousness of the claim.

Adding facts and specific guidance improves the clarity of the information.

Now try this

Using the case of **Kent v Griffiths 2000**, plan the structure of a file note briefing the solicitor advocate to appear in court. You will need to outline the case, explain relevant case documents (claim and defence) and suggest the next steps in the process.

Actus reus – criminal actions and conduct

Murder is the intentional killing of another human being and is an **indictable offence**. There are two key elements in determining criminal liability in a murder case, the first is *actus reus*.

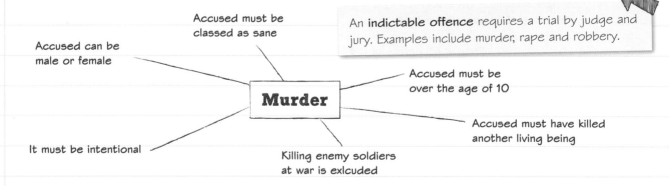

Accused must be classed as sane

Accused can be male or female

Murder

It must be intentional

Killing enemy soldiers at war is exlcuded

Accused must be over the age of 10

Accused must have killed another living being

An **indictable offence** requires a trial by judge and jury. Examples include murder, rape and robbery.

Definition of murder

Below is the description of the 'year and a day' rule defined by Sir Edward Coke (1797). The rule was abolished in 1996, largely because of advances in medicine.

'*Murder is when a man of sound memory and of the age of discretion, unlawfully killeth within any county of the realm any reasonable creature in rerum natura, under the King's peace, with malice aforethought, either expressed or implied by the law, so as the party wounded, or hurt, etc., die of the wound, or hurt, etc., within a year and a day after the same.*'

Sir Edward Coke SL PC was a 17th century English barrister and judge.

Actus reus

Actus reus is a Latin phrase that refers to criminal actions or conduct.

In order to establish the *actus reus* for murder, the actions of the defendant must have led directly to the death of another human being. Legally, a human being must be a living, breathing individual who is not brain dead.

Causation

Causation means that the defendant's actions must have caused death. There are two types of causation.

1. Factual causation uses the 'but for' test – would the death have occurred if the defendant had not acted?

2. Legal causation is an investigation of whether the defendant's act was culpable or blameworthy.

 Key study **R v White 1910**

Scenario: The defendant poisoned his mother's bedtime drink. However, she died in her sleep of natural causes.

Outcome: The defendant had not caused the death. He had intended to kill and carried out an act to cause death, but there was no link with the actual death. The defendant was convicted of attempted murder.

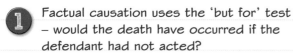 **Now try this**

List three actions that could lead to an unlawful killing.

 How is *actus reus* applied in each case?

Mens rea – intention

The two elements that have to be proved to establish criminal liability for murder are: *actus reus* and *mens rea*. The required *mens rea* is intention.

Mens rea

Mens rea means the intention or knowledge of wrongdoing. It is sometimes referred to as the guilty mind or malice aforethought.

To establish the *mens rea* for murder it must be shown that the defendant intended to kill or cause **grievous bodily harm (GBH)**.

This is different to the motive of a crime which is the reason for an intended action.

> Grievous bodily harm (GBH) is the deliberate serious physical injury inflicted on one person by another.

Intent

There are two types of intent.

 Direct intent

This is where the purpose or desire is to cause death or GBH.

 Indirect intent – sometimes called oblique intent.

This is when the defendant did not intend to cause death but believed that death was virtually certain.

Direct intent

The jury may decide that direct intent existed at the time of the killing and the aim of the defendant was to kill or cause GBH. Other evidence may suggest intention, for example if the defendant made threats to kill or if the killing was pre-planned.

Indirect intent

This relates to situations where the defendant states they did not intend to cause death, but, at the time of the killing, realised death or serious harm would be a virtually certain outcome. For example, a woman sets fire to her flat knowing her mother is in there. Her aim is to claim the insurance but her mother dies in the fire.

Key study **R v Woollin 1999**

Scenario: The defendant threw his 3-month-old baby son onto a hard surface. The baby sustained a fractured skull and died.

Outcome: The jury convicted as it was virtually certain that the defendant knew a 3-month-old baby would die or suffer serious harm. This case provides the current test for indirect intent. The conviction for murder was replaced with a conviction for manslaughter by the House of Lords due to a previous misdirection by the trial judge.

> This case illustrates the distinction between the subjective and objective nature of oblique intent.

 Now try this

> Why is a possible motive different to the *mens rea*?

A man hires a hit man to murder his business partner. The hit man purchases the gun, trails the business partner and shoots them.

Explain the *mens rea* of **both** parties.

Criticism and reform of current law

The law is constantly criticised and under review. Proposals are made for changes to keep up with the needs of modern society.

Issues prompting reform

Law reform can address the following kinds of problems:

- There is no clear definition of murder, as it has developed from common law.
- Some terminology is confusing because it is so old fashioned.
- Advice given to juries on intention has changed often and is confusing.
- Cases vary in detail and the current law can be inflexible when dealing with these differences. For example, there is little discretion between someone intending grievous bodily harm and a serial killer.

Common law

Common law usually refers to past cases that set **precedents** and influence decisions in future similar cases.

Law reform

The Law Commission reviews the law to ensure that it is fit for purpose. In 2004, it referred to the law relating to unlawful homicide as a 'mess'. In the report *Murder, Manslaughter and Infanticide*, published in 2006, it put forward recommendations for reform.

> The Law Commission reviews criticisms
> ▼
> The Law Commission proposes amendments
> ▼
> Parliament accepts or rejects the proposals

Proposals for reform

The Law Commission suggested a new statutory definition of murder and the following reforms to homicide offences.

First degree murder (Mandatory life sentence)	• Killing intentionally • Killing when the offender intended serious injury and was aware of the risk of death
Second degree murder (Discretionary life maximum penalty)	• Killing when the offender intended serious injury • Killing when the offender intended some injury, fear or risk and was aware of a serious risk of death • Killing when there is a **partial defence** to murder
Manslaughter (Discretionary life maximum penalty)	• Killing through gross negligence • Killing as a result of a criminal act with an intention to cause injury or with an awareness of a serious risk of causing injury

Although the suggested definitions and reforms did not move ahead, significant reforms have been made to partial defences.

Murder and voluntary manslaughter

Manslaughter refers to all unlawful homicides that are not classed as murder. Unlike murder, a manslaughter charge does not carry a compulsory life sentence. The sentence is left to the judge to decide. **Voluntary manslaughter** may be used as a **partial defence** to murder.

> 🔗 **Links** To remind yourself about partial defences, see pages 51, 52 and 53.

Now try this

Explain three reasons why the law needs to keep changing.

> Think about changes in society that have prompted changes to the law, such as the sentencing for acid attacks.

Voluntary manslaughter as a partial defence to murder

To reduce a murder charge to voluntary manslaughter, a partial defence such as loss of control must be proved. Partial defences have been transformed by the Coroners and Justice Act 2009.

Voluntary manslaughter

There are two types of manslaughter: **involuntary** (without intent to kill) and **voluntary**.

Voluntary manslaughter is where the *mens rea* has been affected by mitigating circumstances that create a partial defence, leading to the charge of murder being reduced to manslaughter.

Partial defences do not negate the liability of the defendant and will not lead to an acquittal. Partial defences only apply to murder and not to other offences.

 Links To read about involuntary manslaughter see pages 55 to 57.

Partial defences

A partial defence can only be applied to murder with the aim of reducing the charge to manslaughter. There are three partial defences to murder:

1. loss of control (known as provocation before 2010)

2. diminished responsibility

3. killing in pursuance (following) of a suicide pact.

Coroners and Justice Act 2009

The Act resulted in the defence of provocation only being applicable to killings that took place before 4 October 2010. The Act repealed provocation and, after that date, replaced it with **loss of control**.

Provocation before 2010

Provocation was governed by s.3 of the Homicide Act 1957.

The defendant had to be **provoked** by things said, done or both. The defendant had to suddenly and temporarily **lose control**. The provocation had to be such that it would lead to a reasonable person losing control.

Tests for provocation

The jury decide whether a defendant was provoked by using:

1. **a subjective test**: was the actual defendant provoked enough to lose self-control? For example, the defendant felt threatened by the victim.

2. **an objective test**: would the reasonable person have been provoked enough to lose control and do as the defendant did? For example, the reasonable person would have considered the victim's threats as serious provocation.

 Key study **R v Ahluwalia 1993**

Scenario: After years of physical and mental abuse in her marriage, the defendant set fire to her husband, who subsequently died.

Outcome: The defendant was convicted of murder but appealed on grounds of diminished responsibility and provocation. The Court of Appeal determined that she could not claim provocation, as the loss of control was not sudden.

Mitigating factors may reduce the maximum sentence term. For example, if the defendant was a 12-year-old child would they be treated differently from an adult?

Now try this

Outline three factors that you would consider to be 'mitigating circumstances' reducing a murder charge to manslaughter. Give an example for each factor.

Loss of control

Loss of control is now the current and applicable law for partial defences. Prior to 2010 it was provocation.

Key elements of loss of control – after 2010

| Loss of control s.54 and s.55 Coroners and Justice Act 2009 | ▷ | 1 Defendant lost control. 2 There was a qualifying trigger. 3 A person of the same age and sex and with a normal degree of tolerance might have reacted in the same way in the circumstances. | ▷ | Qualifying triggers 1 Fear of serious violence from the victim to the defendant or another. 2 Things said or done or both forming circumstances of an extremely grave nature and that caused the defendant to have a justifiable sense of being seriously wronged. |

Changes

The key points relating to the Coroners and Justice Act 2009 include the following:

- The requirement of 'sudden and temporary' has been dropped. This is wider than the law on provocation.
- The Act introduced qualifying triggers, thereby narrowing the scope of the defence.
- Subjective and objective elements have been retained.

Limitations

Despite the progress of the reform, the Coroners and Justice Act 2009 is not without limitations.

- Sexual infidelity alone cannot be a qualifying trigger.
- The defence is not available to a defendant acting in revenge.
- The defence is not available to a defendant who incited the things said or done or the violence.

Degree of tolerance and self-restraint

This quotation helps to define loss of self-control:

'For the individual with normal capacity of self-restraint and tolerance, unless the circumstances are extremely grave, normal irritations and even serious anger do not often cross the threshold into loss of control.'

L.H. Leigh, 'Clarifying the Loss of Control Defence', *Criminal Law & Justice Weekly*

Now try this

Draw a table outlining and comparing the law on partial defences before and after the changes were made by the Coroners and Justice Act 2009.

Diminished responsibility

Diminished responsibility can be cited due to a mental impairment. This is recognised as a partial defence reducing a murder charge to voluntary manslaughter.

Definition before 2010

This partial defence was defined by s.2 of the Homicide Act 1957 and required abnormality of mind that substantially impaired the defendant's responsibility for their actions or omissions.

Abnormality of mind was given a wide interpretation – both physical and psychological conditions could be included.

Definition from 2010

This partial defence was reformed by the Coroners and Justice Act 2009. The definition is now contained in s.52 of this Act.

Reform of diminished responsibility

The Coroners and Justice Act 2009 has provided a clearer and modern definition of diminished responsibility. Requiring a recognised medical condition has allowed for changes in medical knowledge.

Proving diminished responsibility

What must be proved?	
The defendant had an abnormality of mental functioning.	This means a state of mind so different from other people that it would be considered as abnormal.
It resulted from a recognised medical condition.	The jury is not bound to accept medical evidence but expert psychiatric evidence is very important.
It substantially impaired the defendant's ability to understand the nature of their conduct, or form a rational judgement, or exercise self-control.	This means there must be some causal connection between the defendant's abnormality and the killing, but the abnormality need not be the sole cause. The defence will not be successful if the defendant's abnormality made no difference to their behaviour.

 Key study **R v Golds 2016**

Scenario: The defendant had attacked his partner with a knife at their home in front of her young children following an argument. He had a history of mental disorder leading to outpatient treatment and medication.

Outcome: The defendant claimed diminished responsibility. He was convicted of murder and appealed. His appeal was dismissed by the Supreme Court.

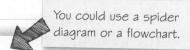
You could use a spider diagram or a flowchart.

Now try this

Draw a diagram of your choice to summarise the relevant points on partial defences from the Coroners and Justice Act 2009.

Reform

Some proposals for reform have been accepted and affect partial defences; others have not been accepted by the Government.

Problems

The Law Commission report *Murder, Manslaughter and Infanticide* stated that the partial defence of provocation was a confusing mixture of case law decisions and statutory provisions. The Commission also noted that the partial defence of diminished responsibility was out of date.

Provocation before 2009

The law before the reforms was said to have a gender bias. Provocation required a 'sudden' loss of control and the law did not recognise provocation that had built up over time. This meant that the partial defence of provocation was less likely to be available to women who are unable to kill using physical strength alone: seeking a weapon implies a delay and therefore the loss of control is not sudden. Sudden loss of control was not recognised in cases where women suffered a period of sustained abuse and their state of mind built up over time (the slow burn).

Fear of violence was not given recognition, although revenge killings and cases relating to sexual infidelity could be included.

Diminished responsibility before 2009

Critics believed that the defence was too widely available and included cases involving extreme jealousy.

The definition of diminished responsibility was very complicated and difficult for juries to comprehend.

The defence mixes legal, medical and moral issues and the jury basically had to decide the issue of 'mad or bad'.

Before 2009, juries had to interpret a complex definition of 'diminished responsibility'.

Reform in the Coroners and Justice Act 2009

- s.52 clarifies and simplifies the definition of the reformed partial defence of loss of control: it requires a recognised medical condition, giving more scope for medical evidence and developments in medical science.
- s.54 drops the requirement of a 'sudden' loss of control. Not applicable to revenge cases.
- s.55 defines the qualifying triggers for the availability of the reformed partial defence of loss of control. Sexual infidelity may be evidence but alone cannot be classed as a qualifying trigger.

Now try this

Read the following fictitious headlines and apply law to each of them.

> **Victim's dismembered body found in cardboard box: defendant 'needed the victim's money to settle gambling debts'**

> **36-year-old man who killed his parents said aliens from space instructed him to do it!**

Think back to *mens rea* and motive. Would the *mens rea* element potentially lead to murder or voluntary manslaughter?

Voluntary and involuntary manslaughter

The main difference between voluntary and involuntary manslaughter is the requirement of *mens rea*.

Voluntary manslaughter

The elements of voluntary manslaughter are:

- *actus reus* – causing death
- *mens rea* – intention but influenced by loss of control, reducing the charge.

Involuntary manslaughter

The elements of involuntary manslaughter are:

- *actus reus* – causing death
- *mens rea* – recklessness, gross negligence or a *mens rea* related to another offence.

Defining involuntary manslaughter

There are two types of involuntary manslaughter.

1 Gross negligence manslaughter

In such cases, death is not intended or desired but occurs through a serious lack of care.

2 Constructive/unlawful act manslaughter

This type of manslaughter is sometimes referred to as constructive manslaughter as liability is built up from the commission of another crime. Sometimes a death is caused during the commission of another offence.

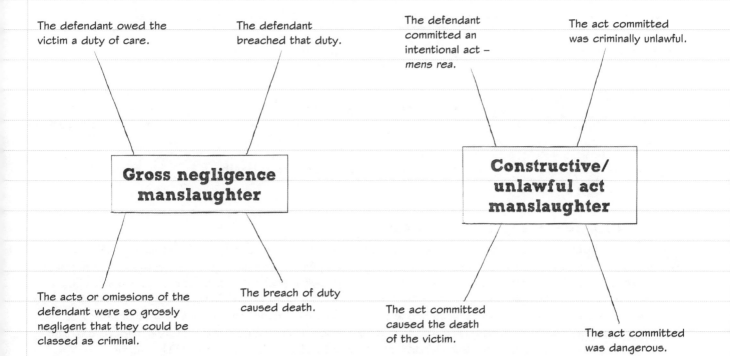

The defendant owed the victim a duty of care.

The defendant breached that duty.

The defendant committed an intentional act – mens rea.

The act committed was criminally unlawful.

Gross negligence manslaughter

Constructive/ unlawful act manslaughter

The acts or omissions of the defendant were so grossly negligent that they could be classed as criminal.

The breach of duty caused death.

The act committed caused the death of the victim.

The act committed was dangerous.

Now try this

Consider how a burglary gone wrong, or a fatal accident caused by a driver texting, fit the types of involuntary manslaughter.

For each type of involuntary manslaughter, outline two scenarios to demonstrate their category. Explain the reasons for your answers.

Unlawful act manslaughter

The unlawful act must be a criminal act; a civil wrong is not enough for liability.

The unlawful act

The defendant must have the *mens rea* for the criminal act, but the prosecution does not need to prove that the defendant intended the result. The defendant need not have foreseen or intended death or harm.

The *actus reus* must be a positive act and not an omission.

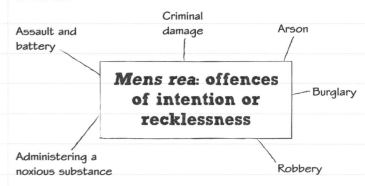

Mens rea: offences of intention or recklessness

- Assault and battery
- Criminal damage
- Arson
- Burglary
- Robbery
- Administering a noxious substance

 Key study DPP v Newbury 1977

Scenario: Two boys threw a paving slab from a bridge as a train approached. The slab went through the window of the cab striking and killing the guard. The boys were convicted of manslaughter but appealed.

Outcome: Their appeal was dismissed by the Court of Appeal so they appealed to the House of Lords with the question: 'Can a defendant be properly convicted of manslaughter, when his mind is not affected by drink or drugs, if he did not foresee that his act might cause harm to another?' The decision was held on the basis that there is no requirement that the defendant foresees that some harm will result from his action.

A dangerous act

An objective test is used to establish whether the act committed was dangerous. There must be a risk of causing some harm to the victim. The type of harm that results does not need to be foreseen.

Mrs Patterson set fire to her house. Motive: to be rehoused.	▶ The unlawful act was arson (*actus reus*) – she intended to cause a fire (*mens rea*).
A friend of her husband was asleep in the back bedroom and died in the fire.	▶ The dangerous act caused death.

Outcome: Mrs Patterson was found guilty of unlawful act manslaughter.

The act must cause death

Factual and legal causation are applied to link the *actus reus* to the death.

Actus reus 🔗 Death

Breaking the chain of causation

The chain of causation can be broken by a new intervening act. For example: a victim is admitted to hospital with a serious stab wound. They are responding well to treatment but, despite their medical records stating that they have a serious nut allergy, hospital staff give the victim food containing nuts. The victim suffers an anaphylactic shock and dies. The stab wound initially was a potential cause of death, but the food containing nuts broke the chain of causation: this was a new intervening act and caused the death. The original defendant (the person who stabbed the victim) could be charged with attempted murder but not with murder, as they did not cause the death of the victim.

Now try this

Apply the elements of unlawful act manslaughter to the following scenario:

Two men broke into a house. They found the car keys for a car parked outside but they were disturbed by the householder. They then fatally attacked the householder while he was trying to protect his car and property.

 Use a diagram or bullet points to identify and apply the key elements.

Gross negligence manslaughter

Gross negligence manslaughter is a form of **involuntary manslaughter** where the defendant is apparently acting within the law.

Similarities

The two types of involuntary manslaughter share some characteristics.

The *actus reus* is causing death.

The defendant(s) did not intend to cause death.

Involuntary manslaughter

Both carry a discretionary sentence.

Death is a result, and legal and factual causation apply.

Differences

Cannot be committed by omission but is constructed upon the commission of another offence.

Unlawful act manslaughter

Elements are unlawful and a dangerous act causing death; *mens rea* for the ulterior criminal offence. E.g. if someone is accidentally killed during a robbery, the defendant must have the *mens rea* of robbery.

Can be an act or an omission.

Gross negligence manslaughter

Elements are duty of care, breach of duty, death and gross negligence for *mens rea*.

Duty of care

A duty to care for another person is sometimes obvious, for example:

- a parent for their children
- a teacher for their students
- a doctor for their patients
- an employer for an employee
- a motorist for other road users.

If a duty of care cannot be easily established the court considers whether it is reasonably foreseeable that the actions of the defendant would cause the death of the victim.

 Key study **R v Adomako 1995**

Scenario: A doctor failed to notice during an operation that a tube had become detached. The patient's brain was starved of oxygen and the patient died.

Outcome: The doctor's actions were classed as gross negligence.

Breach of duty

Breach of duty means the defendant did something the reasonable person would not do, or the defendant failed to do something the reasonable person would do.

Now try this

Explain the difference between a mandatory and a discretionary sentence.

 Remember – the jury decides the verdict and the judge passes sentence using legal guidelines.

Corporate manslaughter

The Corporate Manslaughter and Corporate Homicide Act was passed in 2007, and came into force in 2008.

Before 2008

When a crime requires proof of *mens rea*, for example manslaughter, it is difficult to apply liability to a company.

Prior to the new act coming into force, for a company to be held liable two elements had to be proved.

1 The principle of identification whereby a person has to be found who was the 'directing and controlling mind of the company'.

2 The four elements of gross negligence manslaughter are:

1 duty
2 breach
3 death
4 gross negligence.

🔍 Key study R v OLL Ltd 1994

Scenario: The company arranged outdoor activity holidays for young people. Four teenagers died while canoeing due to lack of supervision.

Outcome: Mr Kite owned the small company and was found to be the directing mind and will of the company. Both Kite and the company were found guilty of manslaughter. The company was fined £60,000 and Kite was sentenced to three years in prison.

Reasons for the new Act

Convictions where a company was responsible for death were very rare. How can *mens rea* be established when a company has no mind? Additionally:

- The larger the company, the more difficult it is to identify the 'directing mind and will'.
- Where more than one person contributed to a dangerous situation, the principle of identification could not work. How can you find one person to blame in a large company?

In the 1980s and 1990s there were several large-scale disasters. It was evident that the companies involved were at fault but the complexity of the principle of identification meant that convictions could not be secured.

In 2008 the law relating to corporate manslaughter was simplified and the principle of identification is no longer required.

After the Southall rail crash in 1997, which killed seven passengers and injured 139, Great Western Trains was fined £1.5 million for health and safety breaches.

Now try this

Outline three ways an employer could be grossly negligent and cause a death in the workplace.

Think about the health and safety considerations a manager should have.

Corporate Manslaughter and Corporate Homicide Act 2007 – elements required

The updated law relating to corporate manslaughter contains provisions about the elements of the offence, investigation, prosecution and penalties.

The offence

The offence of corporate manslaughter requires proof of a serious management failure resulting in a gross breach of duty of care which causes death.

Serious management failure refers to the way the companies' activities are managed or organised.

Failing to provide training and supervision ⟍
Failing to maintain equipment ⟋

Serious management failure

Failing to provide a safe system of work

 R v Lion Steel Ltd 2012

Scenario: An employee, Steven Berry, fell through a fibreglass roof-light to his death. His employers failed to provide proper supervision, training and safety equipment for working at heights.

Outcome: The Cheshire firm admitted to the charge of corporate manslaughter. The company was the third case to be prosecuted under the Corporate Manslaughter and Corporate Homicide Act 2007. The company was fined £480,000.

 R v Cotswold Geotechnical Holdings 2010

Scenario: Alex Wright, aged 27, died while working in a trench investigating soil conditions. The trench collapsed onto him; he suffocated and died at the scene.

Outcome: The jury found that the company's system of work for digging trial pits was 'wholly and unnecessarily dangerous'. This was the first case brought under the new Act. The company was found guilty and a fine of £385,000 was imposed, which the Court of Appeal upheld the next year.

 R v Baldwins Crane Hire Ltd 2015

Scenario: Mr Easton was a crane driver operating a 16-wheel, 130-tonne vehicle when it crashed on a quarry access road. Mr Easton died in the crash. The jury heard that the crane had not been properly maintained and had faulty brakes. The emergency braking system had been disconnected.

Outcome: Baldwin's Crane Hire Ltd was found guilty of corporate manslaughter and was fined £700,000.

Investigation

The police and the Health and Safety Executive investigate allegations of corporate manslaughter.

Now try this

List the pros and cons of the penalties now available for corporate manslaughter.

Remember the prosecution would seek a guilty verdict and would see harsh penalties as beneficial. The defence would seek a lenient fine for the benefit of the company.

Prosecution and penalties

The Crown Prosecution Service makes the decision to prosecute the company.

- Penalties may include unlimited fines, remedial orders and publicity orders.
- The starting point for the level of fine will be determined by the company's turnover – fines could be up to £10 million for large organisations.
- A remedial order requires the company to address the serious management failure and remedy the faults causing death.
- A publicity order requires the offence and fine to be published.

New sentencing guidelines came into force in 2016.

Theft and actus reus

The law of theft is contained in the Theft Acts 1968 and 1978 as amended in 1996. In line with other offences, theft requires proof of *actus reus* and *mens rea*.

Definition

The definition of theft comes from s.1 of the Theft Act 1968. In the Act, s.3 to s.5 deal with the *actus reus* elements.

> 'A person is guilty of theft if he dishonestly appropriates property belonging to another with the intention of permanently depriving the other of it.'

Elements of the *actus reus*

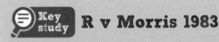

1. Appropriation ▷ 2. of property ▷ 3. belonging to another

Appropriation

This means taking, using, selling or assuming any of the owner's rights. It also covers situations where the defendant has come across the property innocently and later assumes any of the rights of the owner.

 Key study **R v Morris 1983**

Scenario: The defendant switched price labels on goods to pay a lower price.

Outcome: This counted as appropriation as only the owner had a right to interfere with price labels.

Property

The Theft Act definition includes the following:

- **Money and personal property**, for example, mobiles, tablets, jewellery, cars and larger items like container ships.
- **Real property** refers to land and buildings.
- **Things in action** includes things such as debts, a credit balance in a bank account or an overdraft facility.

The element of belonging to another

The property must belong to another. This can be the person who owns the property or has control over it.

Key study **R v Turner (No 2) 1971**

Scenario: The defendant's car was repaired at a garage. When he went to collect it, it had been left outside with the key in. He took the car without paying for the repairs.

Outcome: He was liable for theft of his own car. The car was regarded as belonging to the garage as they were in possession and had control of it.

 Now try this

Draw a mind map explaining the *actus reus* elements of theft.

> The *actus reus* is the guilty act part of the offence.

Theft and mens rea

The *mens rea* is the guilty mind element at the time the crime was committed and for theft, dishonesty and intention must be proved.

Dishonesty

The jury decide whether the defendant was dishonest using a two-stage test known as the Ghosh test.

1 Were the actions of the defendant dishonest by the standards of reasonable and honest people, and if so

2 did the defendant know it was dishonest by those standards?

Defences

There are three examples which would not be dishonest. Where the defendant:

1 believed they had a right to deprive the other of the property, or

2 believed the owner would have consented if they knew, or

3 the person the property belongs to cannot be traced by taking reasonable steps.

Intention

The Theft Act gives two examples of when a defendant will be considered to have intention to permanently deprive the owner of the property:

1 where the defendant intends to treat the property as their own to dispose of without regard to the rights of the owner, or

2 where borrowing or lending is equivalent to an outright taking or disposal.

Motive

If *actus reus* and *mens rea* of theft are established the motive is irrelevant even if it is kind.

A modern version of Robin Hood – stealing from the rich to give to the poor – would still amount to theft.

actus reus: appropriation of property belonging to another	+	mens rea: dishonesty and intention to permanently deprive	=	criminal liability for theft: maximum sentence of 7 years

The British Retail Consortium reported that the cost of retail crime in the UK had risen to £613 million in 2016.

Now try this

Explain how shoplifting and pickpocketing fit into the legal definition of theft.

Robbery 1

Robbery is using or threatening force to commit theft. The maximum sentence for robbery is a life sentence.

Definition

Robbery is defined by s.8 of the Theft Act 1968 as:

> 'A person is guilty of robbery if he steals, and immediately before or at the time of doing so, and in order to do so, he uses force on any person or puts or seeks to put any person in fear of being then and there subjected to force.'

Factors of theft

☑ A completed theft is essential.

☑ Force or the threat of force is essential.

☑ The force or threats can be directed at any person.

☑ The force or threats must be in order to steal and must take place immediately before or at the time of the theft.

Force

Actus reus of theft must be proved – appropriation of property belonging to another.

Threatening or using force to put another in fear of immediate physical violence immediately before or at the time of the theft must also be proved.

The force must be more than, for example, nudging a person. The threat of force can be expressed or implied by gestures.

 Key study **R v Robinson 1977**

Scenario: The defendant was owed £7 by a woman. When he tried to collect the money, he got into a fight with the woman's husband. As they fought a £5 note fell from the husband's pocket. The defendant took it and kept it.

Outcome: He was convicted of robbery and appealed. On appeal, the conviction was quashed citing s.2(1)(a) since the defendant had an honest belief that he was entitled to the money.

Key study **R v Clouden 1987**

Scenario: The defendant snatched a bag from a woman's hands without touching the woman.

Outcome: It was held on the facts that the force used on the bag was enough to amount to force on a person.

Manchester teenager uses umbrella to scare off armed robber at £3 million house

The fact that the robber is armed is an aggravating factor that would lead to a harsher sentence.

Aggravating factors

The Sentencing Council guidelines for robbery include the following aggravating factors:

- level of force or violence
- use of a weapon
- vulnerability of the victim
- number of people involved
- value of the items stolen
- wearing of a disguise, and
- time of the offence.

Now try this

Write a list of mitigating factors that could lead to a lesser sentence for robbery and explain why.

 The Sentencing Council guidelines include an unplanned robbery as a mitigating factor.

Robbery 2

Criminal liability is established when the defendant commits the crime and has a guilty state of mind at the time.

Mens rea

The defendant must have the *mens rea* for theft – dishonesty and an intention to permanently deprive.

The defendant must have the intention or be reckless as to the threat or use of force.

Mens rea for theft   **+**   Mens rea for threat or use of force

Types of robbery

Although robbery is an indictable offence with a maximum sentence of life, for sentencing purposes the guidelines distinguish between the types of robbery.

Robbery	Sentencing
Street/less-sophisticated robberies that take place in public places	Community order: 12 years' custody depending on aggravating and mitigating factors
Professionally planned commercial robberies	18 months' to 20 years' custody depending on aggravating and mitigating factors
Robberies from a dwelling	1 to 16 years' custody depending on aggravating and mitigating factors

 Key study ## R v Murray, Royle and others 2008

Scenario: 'Securitas depot robbery', Tonbridge, Kent. The manager of the depot was kidnapped, and his wife and child were held at gun point. The criminal gang made off with £53.1 million.

Outcome: Seven men were tried and convicted: Murray faced a 25-year prison term; Allen was sentenced to 18 years; Rusha, Coutts and Royle were given indefinite sentences with a 15-year minimum; Hysenaj received a 20-year and Bucpapa a 30-year sentence.

 Key study ## R v Kassaye and others 2010

Scenario: 'Graff Diamond robbery', London. Two smartly dressed men armed with handguns walked into the jewellers and took 43 items of jewellery valued at £40 million.

Outcome: Four men were tried and convicted: Kassaye received a 23-year sentence, and three other men, Buyene, Mogg and Thomas, each received a 16-year sentence.

Now try this

Produce a diagram explaining the aggravating factors in one of the types of robbery from the table above.

The two types of burglary

Section 9 of the Theft Act 1968 as amended provides two separate offences of burglary.

Section 9(1)(a)

A person is guilty of burglary if they enter any building or part of a building as a trespasser with intent to steal, to inflict grievous bodily harm or to do unlawful damage.

Section 9(1)(b)

A person is guilty of burglary if, as a trespasser, having entered any building or part of a building, they steal or attempt to steal, or inflict or attempt to inflict grievous bodily harm.

Similarities

Both offences require entering a building, or a part of it, as a trespasser.

In many cases the same actions could satisfy both offences.

Differences

Section 9(1)(a) can be satisfied with intent to steal or inflict GBH or to do unlawful damage. The intent must be present at the time the defendant enters the building.

Section 9(1)(b) requires the defendant to attempt to steal or to actually steal, to attempt to inflict or to actually inflict GBH. There is no provision in this offence for committing unlawful damage. The intent may be formed after entering the building.

 Key study **Hatton Garden heist**

Scenario: In 2016 a criminal gang were convicted of burglary. Over 2 days they used heavy cutting gear to break into Hatton Garden Safe Deposit Ltd. They made off with gold, diamonds and sapphires worth up to £14 million in holdalls and wheelie bins.

Outcome: John Collins (75) was sentenced to 7 years, while Carl Wood (59), Daniel Jones (61), Terry Perkins (67) and William Lincoln (60) were all sentenced to 6 years. Another man, Hugh Doyle (48), was given a 21-month suspended sentence.

The burglary of the Hatton Garden underground safe deposit facility has been called the 'largest burglary in English legal history'. The picture shows a hole that the gang bored through a concrete wall in order to gain access to deposit boxes.

Now try this

Consider the Hatton Garden heist. Does it illustrate s.9(1)(a) or s.9(1)(b) or both? Explain your answer.

 Check the legal definitions at the beginning of this page.

Liability for burglary

In most cases, this part of the *actus reus* will be obvious. For example, where someone has broken into a house or factory to steal property.

Entry

Entry extends to the physical act of going behind a counter in a shop to take money from the till. It can also include just part of the body entering into a building, for example, smashing a window and reaching inside to steal items.

Defining a building

A building should be reasonably permanent and includes outbuildings such as sheds, garages or greenhouses.

A building may also include inhabited vehicles and vessels, which expands the meaning to include caravans, canal barges and campervans if they are being used as a dwelling.

 Key study R v Ryan 1996

Scenario: The defendant was found stuck in the kitchen window of a home belonging to an elderly man. His head and arm were inside the house but the rest of his body remained outside. The fire brigade had to be called to remove him.

Outcome: He was convicted of burglary. He then appealed on the grounds that there had been no effective entry, but his conviction was upheld.

Key study R v Walkington 1979

Scenario: The defendant was in a department store. Seeing a till partially opened and unattended, he reached behind the counter and looked into the till but it was empty. He was charged with burglary under s.9(1)(a) for entering a part of a building with intent to steal.

Outcome: He was convicted and appealed contending that the counter cannot amount to a part of a building. His conviction was upheld. The counter area was clearly out of bounds to the public and thus he was a trespasser.

Trespassing

A person entering a building is not a trespasser if the owner of the building has given them permission to be there.

The permission may be express or implied, covering a customer's rights to enter the public areas of a shop.

For criminal law, a trespasser must have the *mens rea* for trespass.

The defendant must know or be reckless as to whether they are entering a building without consent.

 Key study R v Collins 1972

Scenario: Collins was charged with burglary after entering a girl's bedroom. She mistook him for her boyfriend and invited him in to have sex. She realised her mistake and screamed; he ran off.

Outcome: His conviction was quashed as, at the time, he did not know he was a trespasser as he thought the girl had invited him inside.

Element	s.9(1)(a)	s.9(1)(b)
Actus reus	Enter a building or part of a building as a trespasser	Enter a building or part of a building as a trespasser and attempt to steal or steal, or attempt to inflict GBH or inflict GBH
Mens rea	Know they are trespassing and intend to steal or inflict GBH or do unlawful damage	Know they are trespassing and intend to steal or inflict GBH

Consider both domestic and business premises.

Now try this

Make a spidergram showing examples of buildings or parts of buildings where a burglary could take place.

Fraud by false representation – *actus reus*

Fraud is where a person is deceived by the fraudster who aims to make a gain – usually financial – or to cause a loss to the other.

Definition

The Fraud Act 2006 provides a definition in s.2. A person is in breach of this section if they:

- dishonestly make a false representation which is untrue or misleading; and
- intend, by making the representation, to make a gain for themselves or another or to cause a loss to another or to expose another to a risk of loss.

Scams

This is an area of massive growth. In the past a person could be deceived on a face-to-face basis or over the telephone. However, the internet has provided many more opportunities for deception. Cybercrime scams involving social media or fake websites are increasingly common.

Growth has also occurred in scams involving mobile phones. Smishing is a specific scam designed to get you to divulge personal information. The message or person calling may assume the role of your bank to encourage you to trust them.

The value of fraud committed in the UK in 2016 topped £1 billion.

Actus reus

The *actus reus* is making a false representation – a representation must be about fact, law or state of mind.

It does not include statements of opinion. The representation could be express – specifically stated – or implied through conduct.

s.3 states that silence can be a misrepresentation where the defendant has a duty to disclose.

False representations made through computers, websites and other forms of modern technology are incorporated into the definition in the Fraud Act 2006.

Collecting money from people for a fake charitable cause would be an example of fraud by false representation.

Now try this

Give three examples of cybercrime and explain the *actus reus* of each.

 'Cat-fishing' is where the offender uses another person's identity on social media to obtain an advantage such as gaining personal details.

Fraud by false representation – mens rea

The *mens rea* is dishonesty and the intention to make a gain or cause a loss to somebody else.

Definition

As fraud is a conduct crime, it does not matter whether a gain or loss resulted.

Three criteria are used to establish the *mens rea* of fraud by false representation. They are:

1 dishonesty

2 intent to make a gain or cause a loss

3 knowledge that the misrepresentation is or might be untrue or misleading.

Dishonesty

The test for dishonesty is the Ghosh test.

 R v Ghosh 1982

Scenario: A surgeon claimed money for operations he had not done. He argued that he was owed the same money for legitimate consultancy fees and therefore his actions were not dishonest.

Outcome: The jury convicted and the surgeon appealed. His conviction was upheld.

Gain or loss

The gain or loss must be intended and can refer to money or other property. The gain or loss can be permanent or temporary.

 See page 61 for more on the Ghosh test.

In the Court of Appeal's decision, Lord Lane CJ explained the dishonesty test as follows:

'In determining whether the prosecution has proved that the defendant was acting dishonestly, a jury must first of all decide whether according to the ordinary standards of reasonable and honest people what was done was dishonest. If it was not dishonest by those standards, that is the end of the matter and the prosecution fails.

If it was dishonest by those standards, then the jury must consider whether the defendant himself must have realised that what he was doing was by those standards dishonest.'

Fraud by false representation

Actus reus
Making a false statement that is untrue or misleading.

+

Mens rea
Knowing the statement is or could be untrue or misleading. Dishonesty and intention to make a gain or cause a loss.

 Now try this

 Use the legal definition, and the *actus reus* and *mens rea*.

List elements to be proved in a case of a woman fraudulently claiming benefits as a single parent despite living with her partner.

Criminal damage

We can find out about cases where property belonging to another has been damaged or destroyed by offences contained in the Criminal Damage Act 1971.

Basic offence

Section 1(1) defines the offence of criminal damage:

> 'A person who without lawful excuse destroys or damages any property belonging to another intending to destroy or damage any such property or being reckless as to whether any such property would be destroyed or damaged shall be guilty of an offence.'

The maximum sentence for criminal damage is 10 years in prison.

Lawful excuses (s.5)

Legally the defendant can present two excuses.

 The defendant believed that the owner had or would have consented to it if they had known.

 The defendant destroyed, damaged or threatened to do it to protect property belonging to themselves or another.

Actus reus
Damaging or destroying property belonging to another.

Mens rea
Intending to destroy or damage property or being reckless.

R v G and another 2003

Scenario: Two boys aged 11 and 12 were camping out overnight. They found some old newspapers in the yard of a shop and set fire to them. They left, thinking the fire would naturally burn out. The fire spread to a wheelie bin and to the shop causing over £1 million of criminal damage.

Outcome: The boys were convicted but appealed. The House of Lords quashed their conviction, confirming that a subjective test is used for recklessness – the boys had to be aware of the risk of the criminal damage occurring.

R v Dudley 1989

Scenario: The defendant threw a petrol bomb at an occupied house, the residents put out the fire and little damage was done. The defendant was convicted of arson.

Outcome: Though the residents' lives were not endangered, the defendant did intend to endanger their lives. He had the required *mens rea* and was convicted of arson.

Aggravated offence

The aggravated (as opposed to basic) offence of criminal damage is contained in s.1(2):

> 'A person ...
> (a) intending to destroy or damage any property or being reckless as to whether any property would be destroyed or damaged; and
> (b) intending by the destruction or damage to endanger the life of another or being reckless as to whether the life of another would be thereby endangered;
> shall be guilty of an offence.'

Differences

The key difference between the basic and aggravated offences is that the aggravated offence includes intending or being reckless as to life being endangered.

Now try this

Ann broke a window to gain entry to her rented house as she had forgotten her key. Is she guilty of an offence?

Explain the reasons for your answer.

 Think about the rules relating to 'lawful excuse'.

Arson

Two further offences are created by the Criminal Damage Act and involve damage or destruction of property by fire.

Basic offence

Section 1(3) of the Criminal Damage Act 1971 creates the offence of arson, which is defined as destroying or damaging property by fire.

A charge of arson may be brought alongside the basic or aggravated offences in s.1(1) or s.1(2).

Actus reus and mens rea

The *actus reus* of arson is the damage or destruction of property by fire.

The *mens rea* is intention or recklessness as to damaging property belonging to another by fire.

Aggravated offence

The offence of aggravated arson in s.1(4) also requires a *mens rea* element relating to endangering life.

The maximum sentence for arson is a life sentence.

Arson is the largest single cause of fire in the UK even without events such as the 2011 riots which destroyed property such as this shop in Tottenham, north London.

Criminal Damage Act 1971

▶ s.1(1) basic offence criminal damage

▶ s.1(2) aggravated offence of criminal damage – as previous plus endangering life

▶ s.1(3) basic offence of arson causing damage by fire

▶ s.1(4) aggravated offence of arson – as previous plus endangering life

Re-read the definitions from the Criminal Damage Act.

Now try this

Derek set fire to a nightclub that he and a silent partner jointly own, knowing that the cleaners were inside the property. He did this to get the insurance money. Is he guilty of an offence?

Explain and give reasons for your answer.

Duress by threats

Duress is when the defendant is put in a situation where they are forced to commit a crime due to fear.

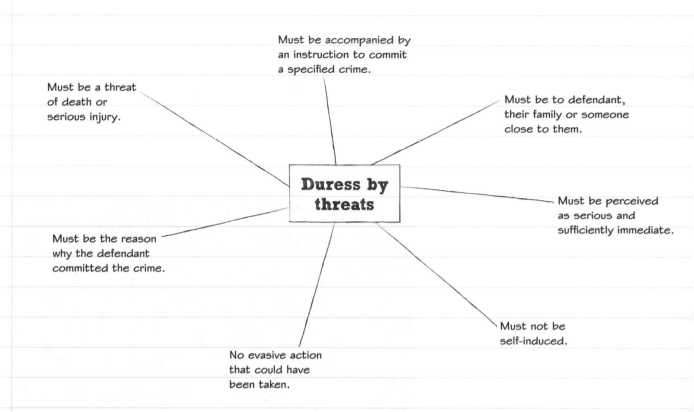

Must be accompanied by an instruction to commit a specified crime.

Must be a threat of death or serious injury.

Must be to defendant, their family or someone close to them.

Duress by threats

Must be perceived as serious and sufficiently immediate.

Must be the reason why the defendant committed the crime.

Must not be self-induced.

No evasive action that could have been taken.

Graham test

A two-part test for duress is contained in **R v Graham 1982**, where Graham claimed that he committed murder with his partner, both under the influence of drugs and alcohol, because he feared him.

1 The defendant must reasonably believe and have good cause to fear the threat.

This stage is subjective but the belief must be reasonable.

2 A sober person of reasonable firmness sharing the defendant's characteristics would have acted in the same way.

This stage is objective but the reasonable person can be attributed characteristics of the defendant such as age, sex, physical or psychological condition.

Limitations

The defence is not available for a charge of murder or attempted murder.

The defence is not available to a defendant who voluntarily and knowingly joined a criminal or terrorist gang or became indebted to a drug dealer.

The defence is not available if the defendant could have taken evasive action.

 Links For more on partial defences see pages 52 and 53.

For more on partial defences see pages 52 and 53.

Now try this

Duress is a complete defence that, if successfully pleaded, leads to an acquittal. Explain how this is different from a partial defence.

 An acquittal means the accused will not be guilty and will be free to leave court.

Duress by circumstances

Duress by circumstances is a similar defence to duress by threats where fear is caused by the actual circumstances.

Relevance

For this defence to be successfully pleaded, the defendant must have been in a situation where they feared death or serious injury, and the circumstances (as the defendant perceived them to be) were such that the defendant had no option but to commit a crime.

 Key study **R v Willer 1986**

Scenario: The defendant was charged with reckless driving. He claimed to have driven in this manner to escape a gang of threatening youths.

Outcome: The Court of Appeal agreed that his actions were 'driven by the circumstances'.

The defence of duress requires six elements, including the expectation that there was no evasive action that the defendant could reasonably be expected to take.

Comparing duress by threats and duress by circumstances

Duress is when the defendant is forced to commit a crime due to fear. The fear may have been caused by threats or circumstances. The table below shows similarities and differences between the defences of duress by threats and duress by circumstances.

Similarities	Differences
The defendant claims that they are not acting of their own free will although they possessed the *mens rea* relating to the crime.	For duress by threats the threat comes from one or more people.
The defendant's actions and state of mind are influenced by fear.	For duress by circumstance, the threat comes from the circumstances surrounding the defendant and the offence.
Both include duress – where a person is put under pressure to commit an unlawful act that they normally would not do.	For duress by circumstance there is no need for the defendant to be told or ordered to commit a crime.
Both are governed by the same tests.	

Elements of defence of duress

The six elements for the defence of duress are:

1 Threat of death or serious injury

2 Threat is directed against the defendant or immediate family or someone close

3 The defendant's perception of the threat and their conduct must be reasonable

4 The defendant's conduct must be directly caused by the threat

5 No evasive action could be taken

6 The defendant must not voluntarily have left themselves open to the threat.

Now try this

You could use bullet points. Keep your points short so that they are easy to remember.

Using a table, list the elements of duress by threats and duress by circumstance.

Intoxication

Intoxication is not a defence itself but can have an impact on *mens rea*, and may affect the outcome of a case.

Definitions

Intoxication is being under the influence of alcohol, drugs (prescribed or otherwise) or other substances, for example, glue.

Voluntary intoxication is where the defendant chooses to become intoxicated.

Involuntary intoxication is where the defendant did not knowingly take an intoxicating substance.

Policy arguments

A policy argument is an argument that assesses a decision in terms of how that decision affects society as a whole.

The **policy arguments** are:

1 The public should be protected from harm or danger caused by intoxicated people.

2 An intoxicated defendant should not be treated more favourably than a sober defendant.

However, criminal liability requires proof of *mens rea*, and intoxication can affect the defendant's state of mind. The aim is to achieve a balance restricting when intoxication can be considered.

Relevance – voluntary intoxication

Intoxication is relevant where all the following points apply:

- voluntary intoxication only
- by alcohol or dangerous drugs
- the defendant lacks *mens rea*
- the crime is one of specific intent.

The charge will be reduced to a lesser offence; if there is no lesser charge, the defendant will be acquitted.

Involuntary intoxication

The courts will assess whether the defendant had the necessary *mens rea*. If they did, intoxication would make no difference.

However, if the defendant was incapable of forming *mens rea*, they cannot be guilty of a basic intent or specific intent crime.

Specific intent crimes

There are different levels of *mens rea* and **intention** is the highest level. Lower levels of *mens rea* are **recklessness** and **negligence**. Specific intent offences require a *mens rea* of intent and nothing less. They are:

- murder
- theft
- robbery
- s.18 Offences Against the Person Act 1861 GBH
- arson with intent.

Basic intent crimes

Basic intent crimes require a *mens rea* of recklessness. If a defendant has become voluntarily intoxicated, their conduct is reckless and therefore they have the required *mens rea*. Basic intent crimes are:

- manslaughter
- rape
- assault and battery
- ABH and arson committed recklessly.

Now try this

Andre is planning to kill his wife, who is having an affair. He buys a knife and a bottle of whiskey, which he drinks to pluck up courage. He then stabs his wife, who dies. Will intoxication affect his case? Explain your reasons for why or why not.

 Consider specific or basic intent, voluntary or involuntary intoxication and the formulation of the *mens rea*.

Self-defence

Self-defence is a complete defence to all offences, if using the statutory defence, and to violent assault, if using the common law defence.

Common law defence

The common law defence is limited to using reasonable force against violent assaults, whereas the statutory defence is to prevent 'any' crime.

A person may use force that will negate the *actus reus* of a crime. This means that the defendant's conduct is lawful, if done to protect:

- themselves
- another, or
- property.

Statutory defence

A separate statutory defence is contained in s.3 of the Criminal Law Act 1967. This allows a defendant to use force to prevent the commission of 'any' offence. This includes violent and non-violent offences, and offences against property.

The statutory defence is wider than the common law defence, but it does require an actual crime being committed.

Key questions

The jury will decide, based on the facts, whether this defence has been established, but there are two key questions.

 1 Given the circumstances, was force necessary?

 2 Was the amount of force used reasonable?

Necessary force

This is judged subjectively, based on the defendant's perceptions of the situation.

If the defendant fears an imminent attack, then reasonable force can be used. Lord Griffith stated in the case of **R v Beckford 1988** that 'a man about to be attacked does not have to wait for his assailant to strike the first blow or fire the first shot, circumstances may justify a pre-emptive strike'.

Reasonable force

There is no definition of reasonable force and the jury must decide whether in the circumstances the force was reasonable. The jury will consider the size, strength and skill of the parties. For the common law defence, the force used must not be disproportionate. In relation to householder cases, the force must not be 'grossly disproportionate'. The householder must be protecting themselves or another and not just defending property.

 **R v Williams (Gladstone) 1987**

Scenario: Williams witnessed a man attacking a youth and went to the youth's assistance. Williams was charged with causing actual bodily harm to the man. It turned out that the youth had mugged the man who had wrestled him to the ground before Williams intervened.

Outcome: Williams was convicted and appealed. His conviction was quashed on grounds that his mistake was a reasonably held mistake.

 R v Martin 2002

Scenario: Tony Martin lived on an isolated farm that had been broken into several times. Two men aged 16 and 30 broke into the farm. On hearing them, Martin took a shotgun and fired into the area where they appeared to be. He shot both men, killing the 16-year-old. He claimed self-defence.

Outcome: Self-defence was rejected as the force used was not considered to be reasonable.

 Now try this

You could use a table format for this activity to distinguish between the common law and statutory defence.

Outline when each defence can be used and explain what must be proved and any limitations for the defence.

Insanity and automatism

Insanity was a popular defence before the abolition of the death penalty. It is now more likely to be raised by the prosecution as insane automatism which is defined below. The defence may seek to rely on sane automatism, also explained below.

Insanity

This defence comes from the M'Naghten Rules (1843). These rules are defined by following the case of Daniel M'Naghten, who tried to kill Sir Robert Peel but mistakenly killed his secretary. In this case, the plea of insanity was successful.

The defence is a defect of reason caused by a disease of the mind so that the defendant did not know the nature and quality of their act and did not know what they were doing was wrong.

Special verdict

If the defendant was insane when the offence was committed, there is a special verdict: not guilty by reason of insanity. If the defendant was insane at the time of the trial and the judge decides they are unfit to plead, the jury then examine the facts relating to the *actus reus* only to reach a verdict.

 Key study **R v Kemp 1957**

Scenario: The defendant suffered from a condition known as hardening of the arteries, which caused a lack of blood supply to the brain and bouts of unconsciousness. In such a state, he attacked his wife with a hammer, causing serious injury.

Outcome: The verdict was not guilty by reason of insanity. A disease of the mind could stem from a physical condition.

Automatism

Lord Denning defined automatism as:

'An act which is done by the muscles without any control by the mind, such as a spasm, a reflex action or a convulsion, or an act done by a person who is not conscious of what they are doing, such as an act done whilst suffering from concussion or while sleepwalking.'

Insane automatism caused by an internal factor	Sane automatism caused by an external factor
▼	▼
Special verdict	Acquittal

Requirements for a successful plea of automatism

A successful plea of automatism as a defence requires the *actus reus* to be an involuntary act and must result from the defendant having a lack of control over their actions. Furthermore, it is dependent on an external factor influencing the defendant, and the state of automatism must not be self-induced.

The defence has been successfully argued in cases involving road traffic offences where a driver lost control of their vehicle during a fit of choking or sneezing.

  Key study **R v Bingham 1991**

Scenario: The defendant was accused of theft for taking a drink and sandwiches without paying. He claimed that he was not fully aware of his actions because he was in a hypoglycaemic state due to low blood sugar levels.

Outcome: The judge claimed that this suggested insanity and the defendant pleaded guilty and later appealed the judges' ruling. On appeal, the defendant's conviction was quashed as his state was a result of an external factor – the insulin – rather than the internal disease of diabetes.

 Now try this

Suggest **one** way in which a state of automatism could be self-induced leading to the loss of the defence of sane automatism.

Self-induced automatism is when a defendant does something or fails to do something that they know will lead to an automatic state.

Stop and search

Stop and search is a tool used by police officers to investigate and detect crime. Their power to use stop and search comes from s.1 of the Police and Criminal Evidence Act (PACE) 1984.

Stop and search

A police officer may stop and search any person or vehicle in a public place if they have reason to believe they are carrying illegal drugs or a weapon, have stolen property or have something in their possession that might be used to commit a crime.

Proper procedure must be followed for all stop and search instances.

Exceptions

For the Terrorism Act, the police do not need to establish reasonable suspicion but a senior officer must authorise the search procedure at particular places and at particular times, and the authorisation must be confirmed by the Home Secretary. Also, reasonable suspicion is not required for s.60 of the Criminal Justice and Public Order Act 1994; police officers may use the power of stop and search where there is a threat of serious violence or public disorder, such as riots or football hooliganism.

Reasonable grounds

Reasonable grounds for stop and search are:

👍 the person is unlawfully in possession of, or has unlawfully obtained, a prohibited article

👍 the person is a terrorist or to prevent an act of terrorism.

Grounds for stop and search cannot be based on:

👎 age

👎 sex

👎 race

👎 religion.

The fact that the police know the individual will not be reasonable grounds for suspicion alone.

The process

The person who is being stopped and searched can only be required to remove outer clothing such as jackets, hats and gloves.

Reasonable force can be used during a stop and search, but only if a person fails to cooperate and only as a last resort.

The person being searched is entitled to a record of the stop and search.

Think about purpose, 'GOWISELY' procedure and reasonable grounds.

Now try this

Outline three reasons why a stop and search could be made and explain the consequences of a stop and search.

Arrest

The police balance an individual's rights to go freely about their business and the need to investigate crime. They have the power to arrest suspects but arrests must be lawful and meet set rules.

Definition

An arrest occurs when the suspect loses their liberty. The person arrested will be cautioned:

> 'You do not have to say anything. But it may harm your defence if you do not mention when questioned something which you later rely on in court. Anything you do say may be given in evidence.'

Warrant for arrest

A **warrant** is an official document signed by a judge or magistrate giving a police officer the right to arrest a person or people named in the warrant. This is used for serious cases.

Most arrests are without a warrant because the police have to act quickly at the scene of a crime.

Lawful arrest

The person being searched and arrested must be involved in, be suspected of involvement in or have attempted involvement in committing a crime.

The police officer must have **reasonable grounds** for believing that it is necessary to search and arrest that person.

Reasonable grounds is a standard based on the facts and circumstances that would lead to a reasonable person suspecting that the person is involved in committing a crime.

Necessity test

Grounds for believing that arrest will be necessary are:

- to discover the person's name and address
- to prevent injury or property damage
- to protect a child or vulnerable adult
- to prevent further offences and to allow for an efficient and prompt investigation of crime.

Proper procedure

On making an arrest, police officers follow proper procedure, which involves:

1 Identifying themselves as police officers

▼

2 Informing the person they have been arrested and the circumstances

▼

3 Explaining why the arrest is necessary

▼

4 Explaining that the person is not free to leave

▼

5 Any necessary searches under s.32(1)

▼

6 Cautioning the person and taking the person to a designated police station as soon as possible.

Failure to follow proper procedure can render an arrest and search unlawful.

Now try this

Make a list of different reasons for arresting a person and explain why reasonable suspicion is needed.

> Think about the police being reactive and proactive. Consider the rights of the suspect and the rights of the general public.

Detention

The purpose of arrest and detention is to allow sufficient time for the police to carry out investigations into suspected criminal behaviour. The Police and Criminal Evidence Act 1984 provides codes of practice to regulate this procedure. The person overseeing a detention is a custody officer.

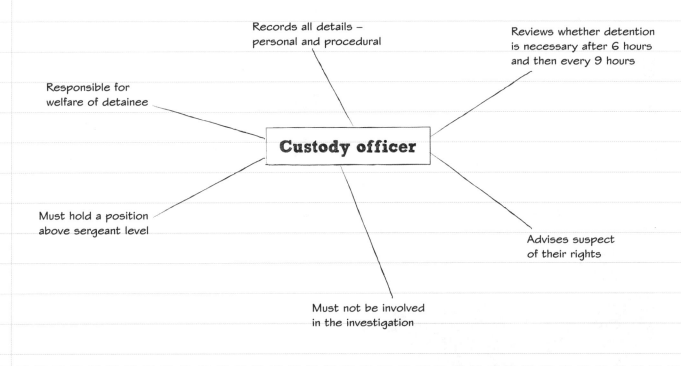

Records all details –
personal and procedural

Reviews whether detention
is necessary after 6 hours
and then every 9 hours

Responsible for
welfare of detainee

Custody officer

Must hold a position
above sergeant level

Advises suspect
of their rights

Must not be involved
in the investigation

Time limits

The basic rule is that a suspect should be charged or released within 24 hours. If the police need more time to continue investigations, the period of detention (custody) can be extended to **36 hours** by authorisation of an officer of at least the rank of superintendent.

Further extensions require a warrant of further detention obtained from a Magistrates' Court; this can extend the detention by 36 hours at any one point and **up to a maximum of 96 hours.**

A person arrested under the Terrorism Act 2000 can be held for **up to 14 days without charge.**

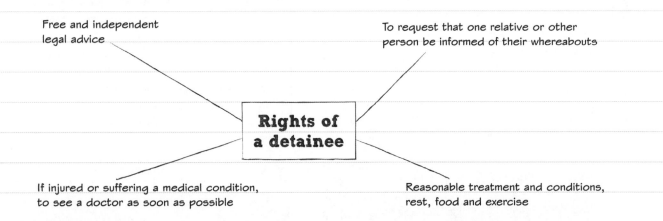

Free and independent
legal advice

To request that one relative or other
person be informed of their whereabouts

**Rights of
a detainee**

If injured or suffering a medical condition,
to see a doctor as soon as possible

Reasonable treatment and conditions,
rest, food and exercise

Now try this

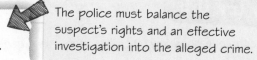

Outline why the right to receive legal advice may be delayed.

The police must balance the
suspect's rights and an effective
investigation into the alleged crime.

Interviews at the police station

A police interview may take place when a person is voluntarily helping the police with their enquiries or when a person is under arrest and the police are trying to ascertain the suspect's involvement in a crime.

The stages of an interview

Generally, there are three stages.

1 The police disclose the allegations to a legal adviser without the suspect being present.

2 The legal adviser consults the suspect in private and in confidence.

3 The interview of the suspect by one or two police officers with the legal adviser present.

All interviews are recorded. More serious cases may have visual as well as audio recordings.

Interview procedure

The suspect will be cautioned before the interview begins. Interviews are recorded on three audiotapes.

1 The first tape is the master copy. It is sealed at the end of the interview and the seal is not broken until the trial takes place.

2 The second tape is a working copy and will be used to produce a transcript of the interview.

3 The third copy is given to the suspect to give to their legal representative.

Responding to questioning

When a suspect is being interviewed, they have three options in response to questioning:

1 to answer questions

2 to provide a prepared statement

3 to respond with 'no comment'.

The Criminal Justice Act 1994 allows the court to draw an **adverse inference** when a suspect remains silent (or responds with 'no comment') before charge, on charge or on trial. The purpose is to discourage the suspect from fabricating a last-minute defence and to encourage speedy disclosure of any genuine defence.

Adverse inference – a legal inference that goes against the concerned party; for example, assuming that a suspect made no comment so that they could fabricate a story.

Special arrangements

Some suspects are vulnerable and need special arrangements.

- If the suspect is aged 10–16, the interview must be conducted in the presence of a parent, guardian or responsible adult.
- Suspects with a mental disability must be accompanied by a responsible adult.
- Suspects who are blind, deaf or unable to speak may need an appropriate adult and/or an interpreter.
- Suspects who cannot understand English will need a translator.

Now try this

Outline three reasons why recording interviews is beneficial.

Recording interviews on tapes provides some protection for both the suspect and the police.

Searches and samples

At the police station, the police can take photographs, fingerprints and DNA samples from the suspect without the suspect's consent. Other body samples require consent and authorisation from a senior police officer.

Fingerprints and DNA

Fingerprint and DNA evidence may be analysed and used to identify a suspect and to link the suspect to the scene of a crime.

DNA and fingerprints are unique to every individual, and cannot be forged. DNA is a molecular and genetic structure present in bodily fluids, hair and skin.

Fingerprints should be obtained as soon as possible after a crime has taken place using the forensic technique of dusting.

Non-intimate samples

Non-intimate samples are defined in s.63 of the Police and Criminal Evidence Act and include saliva, footprints, hair (not pubic hair), sample of nail or from under the nail, and mouth swabs.

The suspect will be asked first if they consent but samples can be taken without consent if there are reasonable grounds to suspect the person has been involved in a recordable offence or if the suspect has been charged.

Intimate samples

Intimate samples are defined in s.65 of the Police and Criminal Evidence Act and include blood, semen, urine, pubic hair and swabs from body orifices other than the mouth.

A medical practitioner must take the intimate sample if an inspector authorises it to prove or disprove a suspect's involvement in a recordable crime.

If the suspect refuses to give consent to providing an intimate sample, this can lead to the court being informed and adverse inferences being drawn.

Forensic science is the application of scientific knowledge and methods to legal problems and criminal investigations to provide objective and logical evidence for a court of law.

Now try this

Explain why advances in forensic science are important to the investigation of crime.

Your Unit 3 set task

Unit 3 will be assessed through a task, which will be set by Pearson. You will need to research the law in relation to information about two cases. You will then be assessed on your ability to explain, analyse and evaluate aspects of criminal law by applying your research on the law to the two cases.

Revising your skills

This skills section is designed to **revise skills** that might be needed in your assessed task.

Problem solving – analyse the task/scenario to identify and explain relevant areas of law. You will evaluate the situation and potential outcomes. Use the IEAAA plan – identify, explain and analyse; apply the law; advise the relevant parties.

Research – identify relevant sources and use the set task information to guide you towards the relevant areas to research and make notes. Remember to use legal definitions, case law examples, legal principles and relevant statute law.

Working under pressure – be well prepared for the external assessment by revising, making notes and planning. Keep calm and be confident in your approach to the assessment.

Set task skills

Communication – use accurate legal and professional terminology appropriate for the target audience. Ensure that your work is legible with correct spelling, punctuation and grammar.

Time management – plan your time carefully. Produce a quick plan to cover all tasks required and to check through your written answers.

Presentation – use the correct format for your written work, as specified in your assessment.

Workflow

In order to research cases and explain, analyse and evaluate aspects of criminal law by applying the law to cases, you will need to:

- read about some cases involving fatal offences and offences against property
- research aspects of law in relation to the offences
- make notes containing details of cases and precedents relating to the offences
- read further information about the offences
- produce documents for members of the legal profession or for clients in relation to the current law relating to fatal offences, property offences and police powers.

Check the Pearson website

The activities and sample response extracts in this section are provided to help you to revise content and skills. Ask your tutor or check the Pearson website for the most up-to-date **Sample Assessment Material** and **Mark Scheme** to get an indication of the structure of your actual assessed task and what this requires of you. The details of the actual assessed task may change so always make sure you are up-to-date.

🔗 **Links** You will find advice on how to approach a fatal offences case on page 82 and guidance on researching a property offences case on page 83.

Now try this

Visit the Pearson website and find the page containing the course materials for BTEC National Applied Law. Download the latest Unit 3 Sample Assessment Material and make a note of:

- the structure of your set task, and whether it is divided into separate parts
- how much time you are allowed for each section of the task
- what briefing or stimulus material will be provided to you
- any notes you might have to make and whether you are allowed to take selected notes into your supervised assessment
- the activities you are required to complete and how to format your responses.

Reading task information

When you are presented with information on two offences, a fatal offence and an offence against property, you must use it to carry out effective research into relevant laws.

Revision task

Below is an article similar to one you may get in your assessment on a homicide offence. You should research the law relating to the article you are given so you are aware of the different types of fatal offences and the circumstances surrounding the case and each victim and defendant.

'Body found in wheelie bin'

The body of a female, who had been fatally stabbed, has been found in a wheelie bin in Dunsop Street. She is believed to be the ex-partner of a 40-year-old man arrested by police in the early hours of yesterday morning. The suspect, who lived in Dunsop Street, is a known drug addict who has struggled with mental health issues. A police spokesman said the female had been the victim of a frenzied attack and that investigations are continuing.

Researching fatal offences

Your research needs to be recent and relevant to the case study you are given. You should:

- research the definitions of murder and voluntary manslaughter and find relevant case law examples
- analyse the offences and any partial defences to decide which will apply
- make notes on the *actus reus* and *mens rea* in the case study. Decide which offence applies and give reasons why
- consider further areas that may relate to the case, for example, potential defences, court proceedings or sentencing.

You are likely to be given a second article regarding a property offence, and you will need to be aware of the law relating to offences against property and police powers as outlined in the article.

Mission Impossible

Three men have been arrested by police whilst making for a getaway car near to Heathrow. The men were carrying rare books worth over £1 million, stolen after entering a warehouse by boring holes in the reinforced skylights in the roof and climbing down 50ft ropes to where the books were being stored. The thieves had avoided motion alarm sensors but a suspicious security guard had alerted the police; they managed to save the antique collection of books and catch all of the perpetrators.

Researching property offences

Your research needs to be recent as well as relevant to the case study.

- Research the definitions of burglary and theft and find relevant case law examples.
- Analyse the offences to decide which offences will apply. Remember that the *actus reus* is the physical element of a crime, and *mens rea* is the mental element of a crime.
- Make notes on the *actus reus* and *mens rea* in the article, considering the planning involved in the offence.
- Decide which burglary offence applies and give reasons why.
- Make notes to define and explain the powers of arrest, reasonable suspicion and necessity.
- Consider theft, burglary, arrest and detention.

Sources of research

Research sources might include:

- articles related to the information given (such as online newspapers)
- textbooks and websites covering fatal offences/property offences
- The Coroners and Justice Act 2009 – extracts containing the requirements of the partial defences/the Theft Acts – extracts containing the legal definitions of relevant offences
- relevant case law noting the legal principle behind the case
- quotes or relevant statistics to use in your conclusion, for example, current homicide rates/ burglary rates from the Office for National Statistics (ONS) website.

This task brief is used as an example to show the skills you need. The content of the task will be different each year and the format may be different.

Now try this

Create a list of subheadings to be used in your research relating to the above case studies.

Researching fatal offences

When finding and reviewing research sources, identify key points that might be useful in your assessed task. Below are two examples of sources that a student has found when researching the first article given on page 81.

Research source 1

This extract is from a report on homicide, compiled by the Office for National Statistics.

Method of killing

As in previous years, the most common method of killing for both male and female victims was by a knife or other sharp instrument, with 186 such homicides (36% of the total) recorded in the year ending March 2015 compared with 204 (39%) in the previous year. This is the lowest number of homicides by knife or sharp instrument since 1993 (182). Although the absolute number of homicides committed by knives or sharp instruments has fallen over recent years, the proportion of homicides committed by this method has only fluctuated slightly from year-to-year as there has been a general downward trend in all homicides. The second most common method of killing was 'kicking or hitting without a weapon', accounting for 95 homicides (18% of the total), a proportion that has remained roughly a fifth over the last decade.

Source: Office for National Statistics

As the first article on page 81 relates to knife crime homicide, this information could be useful for evaluating the success of any defences. For example, it could be said that it is important that such crimes are dealt with strictly to deter others because many deaths are caused by this method – 186 in 2014 to 2015.

Compared to the previous year, the trend for knife crime homicides has decreased but the number of victims is still significant.

'Kicking or hitting without a weapon' – this information is not useful because the case study is about a knife crime homicide.

Identifying key points

Key points that are useful to identify in relation to a source and report might include:

- knife crime homicides (36% of the total)
- trends (lowest number of homicides committed by sharp instruments since 1993)
- statistics (kicking or hitting accounted for 95 homicides (18% of the total)).

Research source 2

This extract is taken from the Crown Prosecution Service (CPS) website.

This information can be found in s.52, and this definition is the important one because it is the definition of diminished responsibility currently used.

The definition of abnormality of mental functioning is relevant to apply to the scenario on the previous page, 'Body found in wheelie bin'.

Knowledge and understanding of a defendant's medical history could determine their liability for the crime.

The case – **R v Sanders 1991** – illustrates the point being made: the jury are not bound to accept medical evidence but it is important.

Section 52 of the Coroners and Justice Act 2009 (the Act) replaces the definition of diminished responsibility as contained in the Homicide Act 1957. This will apply to defendants charged with murder where the acts or omissions resulting in the death of the victim took place on or after 4 October 2010.

The Act creates new subsections namely (1), (1A) and (1B) and outlines circumstances where a person is not to be convicted of murder.

Abnormality of mental functioning means a state of mind so different from that of ordinary human beings that the reasonable person would term it abnormal. It covers the ability to exercise willpower or to control physical acts in accordance with rational judgement. It is a question for a jury.

The jury is not bound to accept medical evidence: *R v Sanders* [1991] Crim LR 781. However, the new wording after its amendment by s.52 gives significantly more scope to the importance of expert psychiatric evidence.

Now try this

Research the legal definition for insanity and outline the key points to be proved.

Researching property offences

When finding and reviewing research sources, identify key points that might be useful in your assessed task. Below are two examples of sources that a student has found when researching the second article given on page 81.

Research source 1

In this extract from 'Oh My *Ghosh*, a Two-part Test for Dishonesty?' from the *Criminal Law and Justice Weekly*, **Ghosh** 1982 devised a two-stage test where 'dishonesty' is uncertain. It is useful when thinking about article 2 on page 81.

Although 'dishonesty' has no statutory definition, *Ghosh* [1982] EWCA Crim 2 devised a two-stage test where 'dishonesty' is uncertain: 1) Was the defendant's behaviour dishonest by the standards of ordinary reasonable and honest people? If no, the defendant is not dishonest. If yes, part two applies; 2) Did the defendant realize his behaviour was dishonest by the standards of ordinary reasonable and honest people? If no, the defendant is not dishonest and, if yes, the defendant is regarded as dishonest. Still, it is only a common law test. Legislation is required. Although the Ghosh test is appealing, flaws have surfaced – it is uncertain and vague, contrary to the principle of certainty of law, violating art.7(1) of the European Convention of Human Rights (ECHR). *Kokkinakis* v. *Greece* [1993] ECHR 20 held: art.7 embodies several important principles, including only law can define offences, prescribe penalties and laws must be defined clearly; the test allows criminalization of the morally wrong as juries decide the reasonable and honest person's standards, leading to inconsistency nationally; and cases with identical facts could reach drastically different results, posing problems regarding certainty of law.

To establish *mens rea*, dishonesty must be established. The defendant's actions were dishonest as they entered via the roof: reasonable and honest people would see this as dishonest. An objective test looks at how members of the public would perceive the actions of the defendant.

The jury will also look at whether the actual defendants who entered the warehouse knew that their actions were dishonest (a subjective test). The three men in the scenario knew they were not allowed to be in the warehouse and they avoided sensor alarms.

The test comes from precedent rather than an Act of Parliament: it has changed over time as different decisions have been made. If the test was enshrined in an Act, it would be more certain, though open to the interpretation of the judge when advising the jury.

Juries are made up of people chosen at random with different views and opinions influenced by culture, geographical area, etc. They decide on the standard, meaning that there could be an inconsistent approach in applying the law.

Identifying key points

Key points that are useful to identify in relation to a source and report might include:

- the Ghosh test
- how the test is applied
- criticism of the test.

The people described in the 'Mission Impossible' article on page 81 entered the building, a warehouse, by boring holes in the skylights and descending by ropes. Their entrance to the building was not legitimate: trespassing is entering the building without permission or authorisation. This is one constituent of the *actus reus*.

The three men were arrested carrying rare books taken from the warehouse: the purpose of entering the warehouse was to steal. Intention forms a constituent of the *mens rea*.

The defendants intended to steal and in fact did appropriate the books. Only the owner of the books had a right to move them, hence s.9(1)(a) and (b) are satisfied.

The main offences are theft and burglary. Committing criminal damage can also be an aspect of the offence as the skylights were damaged.

Research source 2

The definitions of the burglary offences are contained in s.9 of the Theft Act 1968.

This is an extract from s.9 of the Theft Act 1968.

(1) A person is guilty of burglary if—

(a) he enters any building or part of a building as a trespasser and with intent to commit any such offence as is mentioned in subsection (2) below; or

(b) having entered any building or part of a building as a trespasser he steals or attempts to steal anything in the building or that part of it or inflicts or attempts to inflict on any person therein any grievous bodily harm.

(2) The offences referred to in subsection (1)(a) above are offences of stealing anything in the building or part of a building in question, of inflicting on any person therein any grievous bodily harm therein, and of doing unlawful damage to the building or anything therein.

Now try this

Find the legal definition for theft from the Theft Act 1968 and identify the *actus reus* and *mens rea* elements.

Making notes

Compiling clear notes that distil key information you have researched will help you to write a report, a letter, a presentation, or compile case notes. Check with your tutor or look at the most up-to-date Sample Assessment Material on the Pearson website to find out if you can take any preparatory notes into your supervised assessment.

Focus your notes

Do:

- 👍 use bullet points.
- 👍 make relevant notes – they should relate to the task.
- 👍 Make sure your research relates to the law of England and Wales. When searching on the internet always type in what you want to find out about followed by 'UK'; for example, 'Corporate manslaughter UK'.
- 👍 include key facts and figures from your research.
- 👍 use a legal dictionary for legal terms and definitions.
- 👍 use tables of cases/statutes (Acts of Parliament) found in most law books. They are listed alphabetically.

Do not:

- 👎 write pages of notes – condense them into important points.
- 👎 copy large chunks of information from your research.
- 👎 change legal terminology – legal terms have existed for years so if, for example, you change 'the Golden Rule' of statutory interpretation to 'the Brilliant Principle', it will not make sense. Be careful to use legal terminology in the correct context – a defendant in a civil case is not 'guilty' but is 'liable'.

Sample notes extract

- Sections 54 and 55 of the Coroners and Justice Act 2009 cover loss of control.
- Case notes – **R v Ahluwalia 1993**
- Murder carries a mandatory life sentence. Mitigating circumstances may affect the minimum term to be served.
- In **DPP v Camplin 1978**, Lord Diplock stated: '... the reasonable man... is a person having the power of self-control to be expected of an ordinary person of the sex and age of the accused, but in other respects sharing such of the accused's characteristics as they [the jury] think would affect the gravity of the provocation to him...'

Notes on a fatal offence

- Note taking can be in shorthand, such as s.54 and s.55 and CJA 2009.
- Highlight key terms and legal terminology.
- Facts must be relevant. The important thing is the point established by the case – the legal principle.
- Quotes may be used to supplement your discussion and application of the law in the assessment.

Sample notes extract

- The *actus reus* of theft includes appropriation of property belonging to another.
- Case notes – **R v Ghosh 1982** established a two-stage test for dishonesty. Subjective and objective.
- The maximum sentence for burglary of a non-domestic dwelling is 10 years in prison.
- Crown Prosecution Service (CPS) sentencing guidelines.
- 70% of all police-recorded crime in 2014–15 consisted of property offences.

Notes on a property offence

- Use abbreviations. For example, rather than *actus reus* you could use AR.
- Ensure the notes you take are relevant to the information you have already been given.
- Keep in mind that the task may require you to advise clients or members of the legal profession. Think about any terminology that would need explaining to a client.
- Facts and figures, and names of specific cases, are an effective way of supporting your work and establishing your argument or confirming your decisions.

Now try this

1. Make a list of key terms and legal terminology relating to fatal offences. Choose **three** and explain them as if you were talking to a client.

2. Research the defence of duress by threats and make notes on the information you find using the tips listed above.

Reviewing further information: fatal offences

If you are given further information relating to a case you have researched, read it carefully and identify key points to help you prepare documentation on the case.

Homicide

You have been given a two-week placement with a firm of solicitors called Cartmell and Done, working in the criminal department. You are working with colleagues to represent Mr Kennedy, who is charged with murder. You have to prepare a report on the case for your line manager, the firm's criminal law partner. The facts of the case are:

- Colin Kennedy, 40, of Dunsop Street, has been charged with the murder of his ex-wife, Marianna, who was found in a wheelie bin. She had suffered from a savage attack and died from stab wounds to the head and chest.

- The couple had parted two years ago, though Mrs Kennedy had made several complaints that she was being stalked by her former partner.

- In court, it has been alleged that Mr Kennedy was not aware of his actions on the night in question as he had been taking drugs and alcohol.

- It has also been suggested that he had fits of jealous rage and had mental health problems. The trial continues.

Identifying key points

When you read the further information, you need to identify the key points. In this example, they would be:
- ☑ murder
- ☑ voluntary manslaughter
- ☑ partial defences
- ☑ intoxication and insanity.

Explain the legal definition of murder and the *actus reus* and *mens rea* required.

Not aware of his actions – possibly links to insanity or intoxication through drugs and alcohol.

Could a jealous rage cause loss of control? Mental health problems could be a factor linked to loss of control.

Note that some tasks may have a time constraint and you will need to manage your time carefully to give the best possible answer.

Responding to tasks

When responding to tasks, your answers will need to show key skills and qualities in response to command words.

Identify
Indicating the main features of something by recognising it.

Analyse
Presenting the outcome of a detailed and methodical examination, breaking down a situation or scenario, and studying the interrelationships between the parts.

Explain
Showing clear details and giving reasons or evidence to support an opinion or argument.

Command words

Evaluate
Drawing on varied information, themes or concepts to consider, for example, strengths or weaknesses, advantages or disadvantages, alternative actions, and significance; leading to a conclusion or supported judgement.

Illustrate
Including examples to show what is meant.

Apply
Establishing some relationship or connection, as in the application of a rule or principle to a case or fact.

Now try this

List the key points from the partial defences in the Coroners and Justice Act 2009 to be applied to the further information about the homicide.

Structuring a report

If you are asked to write a report, make a plan first so that you use a clear and logical structure. It will help you to use and apply the information from your research.

If you are asked to provide a report on the homicide scenario, your considerations might include:

- explanation of the relevant fatal offences, using professional language and legal terminology
- application of relevant case law and statutes
- analysis of any potential defences applicable
- evaluation of whether any defences will be successful.

Planning a report

You need to plan your report format carefully so that you include all the relevant information for the recipient. The report should be easy to read and have a logical order. Use subheadings to separate the different areas being discussed, and remember to use an introduction and a conclusion.

Below is one structure you could use when planning a report on the homicide case explored on previous pages.

1. Title of the report	Short title, who it is for and who wrote it; include the date	Example: A report on the charges against Mr Kennedy. This report is for the senior criminal law partner of the law firm Cartmell and Done, written by [your name] on [today's date].
2. Introduction	Summary of the facts in the scenario, purpose of the report identifying 3 or 4 key issues	Example: Mr Kennedy has been accused of murder. This report will consider how to establish liability, alternative charges, potential defences and the likely outcome of the case.
3. Numbered sections	Explain offences; apply case law and statutes; analyse possible defences and evaluate. Use subheadings. Deal with scenario in chronological order.	Example: [define – explain – apply] Section 1: Murder definition, *actus reus* and *mens rea*. Coke's definition: (i) age of discretion: Mr Kennedy = adult capable of *mens rea*; (ii) defendant of sound memory (legally insane person not capable of forming *mens rea*). Mr Kennedy unlikely to be classed insane using strict rules of McNaghten test. Section 2: Defence of intoxication. Voluntary taking of drugs/alcohol; reckless but may have impact on a charge of murder. Murder = specific intent crime where *mens rea* must be intention – nothing less will do. If intoxication accepted by jury, lesser offence of voluntary manslaughter possible; could mean Mr Kennedy not subject to life sentence. Section 3: Defence of loss of control. Abnormality of mental functioning, from recognised medical condition that substantially impaired defendant's ability to understand nature of his conduct, or form a rational judgement, or exercise self-control.
4. Conclusion and recommendations	Summarise the main findings, justify potential outcomes and make relevant recommendations.	Example: Section 5 of the report showed that Mr Kennedy may have a defence as he was under the influence of drugs and alcohol; this would only be successful if... as illustrated in...

Now try this

Make a list of subheadings you could use for the case of Mr Kennedy for the main body of the report.

Using your plan to write a report

If you are asked to write a report, use your plan to help you structure it logically and concisely. Remember to use and apply the information from your research. Below is a sample extract from one student's report based on the homicide case explored on the previous pages.

Use subheadings and numbered sections in your reports.

Consider the case study from the perspectives of the prosecution and the defence. How might the perspective of one help the other to establish a defence or a descendant's liability?

Try to use established definitions or parts of definitions and explain them, applying the law to the case study as you go along.

You could use a case such as **R v White 1910** to illustrate factual causation. Make sure that all the case law examples used come from England and Wales.

Your report would continue to explain and analyse the defence case for voluntary manslaughter and the possible impact of the defendant being unaware of his action – intoxication, diminished responsibility, insanity.

Sample response extract

1. Murder

Case for the prosecution: the prosecution barrister will aim to establish liability for murder on the part of the defendant.

1(a) Legal definition

Murder was defined by Coke LJ under the common law and is basically an intentional killing by a person 'of sound memory and of the age of discretion'. This means the defendant must not be under 10 years of age and must be classed as legally sane.

Kennedy is over the age of 10 and the prosecution will seek to prove that he is not legally insane.

1(b) Actus reus

The actus reus (prohibited act) is causing death. Factual and legal causation will be required and the prosecution will use evidence such as DNA and blood samples to link the defendant to the scene of the crime.

1(c) Mens rea

The mens rea (guilty mind) to be proved is intention, which may be direct. For example, if there were witnesses who claimed the defendant had threatened to kill the victim or if there was evidence of pre-planning. Here the stalking of the victim may be linked to the killing.

The other type of intention is where the defendant desired another outcome. For example, to frighten the victim, but their actions were such that would be virtually certain to lead to death or serious injury as in **R v Woollin 1999** – this is referred to as indirect or oblique intent.

This report should continue to a conclusion – it is important to summarise the main findings, justify any potential outcomes and make relevant recommendations.

Now try this

Assuming Mr Kennedy is found guilty of murder, write a brief conclusion with justification for the consequences. Think about the verdict, the sentence, minimum tariffs and whether the law on fatal offences is effective.

Writing a report: appropriate terminology

It is important to use appropriate terminology, format and legal authority in a report.

Sample response extract

To establish criminal liability on a charge of murder, there are two essential elements to be proved – the *actus reus* and the *mens rea*. In the scenario, the accused stabbed the victim several times; this is the *actus reus* that caused death.

1(d) Causation

Factual causation illustrated in the case of **R v White 1910** is evident as, had it not been for the stab wounds, the victim would still be alive. In addition, legal causation is established as the stab wounds were the operative and substantial cause of death. The scenario showed that the accused had threatened to kill the victim on the previous day; this could be evidence of the required *mens rea*. This is intention to kill or to cause grievous bodily harm.

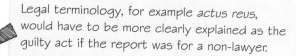 Legal terminology, for example *actus reus*, would have to be more clearly explained as the guilty act if the report was for a non-lawyer.

The law relating to fatal offences is being applied to the scenario.

It is important to use concise explanation and application due to the time constraints. A case law illustration has been used. A brief outline of the facts of a case illustration may be used but keep it short – you need time for including all the relevant factors for the whole of the assessment.

Make sure that you use the details of the scenario to apply the law.

Sample response extract

1. Partial defences

The common law definition of murder requires that the defendant be of 'sound memory' (Coke 1797). This means that the defendant must not be classed as insane. However, some medical conditions can lead to a partial defence of loss of control, as introduced by the Coroners and Justice Act 2009. Diminished responsibility defined in s.52 requires:

- an abnormality of mental functioning
- caused by a recognised medical condition
- substantially impairing the defendant's ability – all points apply to the accused.

A partial defence is likely and is beneficial to the defendant because it reduces a charge of murder to voluntary manslaughter. A murder charge carries a mandatory life sentence but for voluntary manslaughter the sentence is at the discretion of the judge.

Using quotes is a good idea. Make sure you use quotation marks and include reference to the source.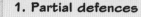

Use bullet points to clearly summarise requirements of an offence or defence and to relate the points to the scenario.

It is important to consider different consequences and to recognise advantages for the defendant, indicating the likelihood of success without being too specific because, in court with trial by jury, a decision can go either way.

Now try this

Select a key study referenced within Unit 3. Write a list that you could use to help you compile a report explaining and applying the relevant law.

Reviewing further information: property offences

If you are given further information relating to details of a case you have researched, read it carefully and identify key points to help you prepare documentation. You will need to use and apply the information from your research if you are asked to produce case file notes, for example in a property offence scenario.

Property offences

In your work in the criminal department of solicitors' firm Cartmell and Done, you have been asked to prepare a summary of the case of Andy Davies, Patrick Davies and Alexei Stollinski, clients who have been charged with several property offences. The facts are as follows:

- Three men, Alexei Stollinski, Andy and Patrick Davies, have been charged with burglary and are being tried at Greathrow Crown Court.

- It has been alleged that the three men plotted to steal over £2 million of rare and antique books.

- Mr Stollinski has complained that he was only involved as he was being threatened by the Davies brothers because he owed them a considerable amount of money.

- Mr Stollinski also complained that he was not given immediate access to a phone call or legal advice at the police station and that he had been intimidated in the police interviews. The trial continues.

If your task has a time constraint, you will need to manage your time carefully to give the best possible answer.

Identifying key points

When you read any further information on a property offence, you need to identify any additional key points. In this example they would be:

- ☑ burglary
- ☑ defence of duress by threats
- ☑ Police and Criminal Evidence Act (PACE) 1984 codes of practice
- ☑ arrest and detention including interviews.

Burglary is a relevant offence, triable either way, so it is heard in the Crown Court.

Theft as a part of burglary needs to be given a full explanation.

Suggests a potential defence of duress by threats.

The rights of a detainee under the PACE codes of practice need to be discussed and justified.

Why use case file notes?

Case notes and case comments are used by legal practitioners to gain an insight into how the law is applied and how judicial decisions are made.

Case notes and comments allow you to:

- put the case in context
- apply the law
- explain the significance of the case
- include legal arguments and counterarguments.

If you are providing case file notes on the scenario, you might include:

- explanation of the relevant offences, using professional language and legal terminology
- application of relevant case law and statute
- analysis of any potential arguments or defences applicable
- evaluation of the potential outcome of the case and/or the area of law in question.

Formatting and structuring case file notes

There is no prescriptive format but case file notes and comments need to be clear, concise and informative.

Below is an example of a structure you could use to compile case file notes and comments.

Title

Catchwords – identifying relevant areas of law; three or four chronological points that will guide your case notes

Narrative – facts, law applied, similar cases, issues

Conclusion – likely outcome, evaluation of the relevant law and procedure

Now try this

Review actus reus and mens rea on pages 48 and 49.

Outline and explain the elements of theft that you would include in the case notes.

Writing case file notes

In order to write case file notes, you will need to use your communication skills to produce accurate, clear and concise notes. Below is an extract from one learner's case file notes on the property offence case explored on the previous pages.

Sample response extract

The defendants are Andy Davies, Patrick Davies and Alexei Stollinski and their case is to be held at Crown Court as it is a serious case. If the defendants plead guilty then sentencing will follow whereas if they plead not guilty it will progress to a trial by jury.

The offence is burglary as set out in s.9 of the Theft Act 1968. There are two separate offences set out in s.9(1)(a) and s.9(1)(b). The offences require the defendant to enter a building or part of a building as a trespasser – this forms the *actus reus*. In R v Ryan (1996), the defendant was found stuck in the opening of the kitchen window in the home of an elderly man. Only his head and one arm were inside the property. The fire brigade had to remove him. He was convicted of burglary. The defendants entered the warehouse as trespassers.

The *mens rea* in this case is that the defendants must know that they are trespassing and must have an intention to steal and for s.9(1)(b) they must steal.

Always use capital letters for the name of an Act and include the year.

You will need to summarise how the law applies to the scenario. Try to use case law examples, statute, quotes and statistics where relevant to justify the points you are making.

Incorporate relevant case law and statute.

This is a good example of using case law to support the argument that entering part of a building is sufficient to establish the *actus reus*.

Avoid using irrelevant information. For example, Stollinski complained about detention and interviews, so you don't need to discuss stop, search and arrest.

Plan carefully so that you have enough time left to include a comprehensive conclusion.

Now try this

Produce catchwords for case notes relating to:

1 a case of arrest for criminal damage and arson.
2 a case of stop and search and a young man being in possession of stolen goods.

Formatting a solicitor's letter

If you are asked to draft a professional letter, you will need to carry out careful research and planning and use your communication skills to produce accurate, clear and concise information that is appropriate for your recipient.

A professional letter

A formal letter needs to be:

👍 in the correct format
👍 short and to the point
👍 relevant

👍 free from spelling and grammatical errors
👍 polite
👍 well presented.

Essential features of a solicitor's letter

Summers and Wood Partners
53 High Street
Bedlam
West Sussex
BG7 9BS

Mr Bailey
Protocol UK Ltd
75 Brooke St
Bedlington
West Sussex
BH5 3BS

5 May 2018

Dear Sir [or] Dear Mr Bailey

Ref. Request for information on Corporate Manslaughter

Yours faithfully [or] Yours sincerely

M. J. Summers

Put your address here – you do not need the phone number or email address. If you are writing on behalf of a law firm, and you have been given the name of the firm but not the address, make one up. (The same would apply to the recipient.)

Place here the recipient's name and address (who you are writing to).

Ensure you include the date – if you have not been given a date, use the current date.

Use the correct salutation – it should be 'Dear Sir' if you do not know the client's name *or* 'Dear Mr Bailey' if you do.

Include the subject of the letter – put it in bold or underline it, and ensure it is on a line of its own.

The text of the letter, written in short, clear paragraphs, would be written by you here. Do not use slang or text speak. If you are writing to a client explain any legal terminology or abbreviations.

Ending – if you have used 'Dear Sir' at the start, use 'Yours faithfully' here; if you used 'Dear Mr Bailey' at the start, use 'Yours sincerely' here.

Type your name below your signature.

Do not forget to proofread for spelling, grammar and punctuation.

Now try this

Select five potential abbreviations of legal terms and provide explanations for a lay person.

Writing a solicitor's letter to a client

Solicitors deal with private and corporate clients and, although email and telephone communication are often used, letters remain a valuable form of communication. Letters could also be presented as a form of evidence, so accuracy and attention to detail are crucial.

> You have managed to gain a placement at a law firm called 'Summers and Wood Partners'. One of the senior partners has asked you to draft a letter to a corporate client, Mr Bailey, the managing director for a local engineering firm, Protocol UK Ltd.
>
> The client is worried as there have been several health and safety breaches at the company and he is concerned that a fatality could occur. He has asked for information on corporate manslaughter as he wants to take proactive steps to prevent this happening.

Sample response extract

Use of an appropriate salutation.

The purpose of the letter is clearly outlined.

The definition of corporate manslaughter is providing context to the rest of the information.

Dear Mr Bailey,

Ref. Request for information on Corporate Manslaughter

Thank you for your request seeking information on corporate manslaughter and criminal liability. Please find the relevant law and potential implications in the text below.

Corporate manslaughter is a statutory offence outlined in the Corporate Manslaughter and Corporate Homicide Act 2007; it affects all companies in England, Wales, Scotland and Northern Ireland.

Including references to case law illustrates the impact of liability on the wider business.

Criminal liability can be imposed where a fatality is caused by serious management failures resulting in a gross breach of duty of care. There is no legal definition of 'serious management failure' but examples include: failure to provide proper supervision and training as in R v Lion Steel (2012); providing defective equipment or vehicles as in R v Baldwins Crane Hire Ltd (2015); failure to provide a safe system of work as in R v Cotswolds Geotechnical Holdings (2011). In each of these cases the companies were liable for corporate manslaughter. The implications for the companies are massive fines, bad publicity damaging their reputation and possibly insolvency.

The learner has clarified who would be responsible should an incident occur and what the employer's duty of care is.

Senior management is defined in s.1 of the Act as 'persons who play a significant role in the management of the whole, or a substantial part, of the organisation's activities'.

An employer has a duty of care, for example, for employees, clients, visitors and members of the public. When considering a gross breach of the duty of care, the jury will consider the seriousness of the situation, the risk involved, breach of health and safety laws, guidance received by the company, and company policies and practices. The breach must be directly linked to the management failure.

Outlining the process of investigation and prosecution and detailing financial penalties serves to underpin the seriousness of health and safety violations.

When a workplace fatality occurs the police take the lead in the investigation along with the Health and Safety Executive (HSE). The police have the powers of arrest and refer the case to the Crown Prosecution Service (CPS), which makes the decision whether to prosecute the company. The implications of legal action are the costs for legal fees and, not least, the time and stress involved.

If a prosecution is successful, penalties include unlimited fines, remedial orders and publicity orders. A remedial order requires the company to address the serious management failure that caused the fatality, and the publicity order requires the company to publish the fact that it has been convicted, the offence, the fine and the terms of the remedial order. The Sentencing Council issues guidelines and considers the turnover of the company in order to provide a starting point for a fine; for example, for a small organisation with a turnover of £2 million to £10 million, the starting point will be between £540,000 and £800,000.

- The letter provides a comprehensive response to the client's query.
- The letter has been carefully structured.
- The learner has used formal but concise language.
- Legal terms and language have been clearly explained and no assumption of prior knowledge has been made.

It is pertinent to mention that, in addition to corporate liability, a director can also attract personal liability and be subject to a prison term and disqualification as a director; this was the outcome in the case R v Sherwood Rise Ltd (2016).

Additional guidance provides information on the personal liability of a director, together with reference to illustrate case law.

Now try this

The above letter needs a conclusion and signature; make a list of points you would include in the conclusion.

Applying the law: police powers

Police officers need to be able to carry out certain procedures in order to detect and investigate crime; these procedures are governed by the Police and Criminal Evidence Act (PACE) 1984. You need to be familiar with the Act and the codes of practice to apply the law relating to police powers.

PACE codes and powers

1 PACE s.1 defines the power of stop and search dealt with in code A.

2 PACE s.24 determines when an officer can make an arrest without a warrant and s.32 deals with search on arrest, power of arrest – code G.

3 PACE s.34 and subsequent sections deal with detention, treatment and questioning – code C.

4 Codes E and F deal with the recording of interviews.

Think about it

1 For **stop and search** think about where, why and how a search can take place and reasonable grounds for a stop and search.

2 For **arrest**, think about the two main criteria: 1) that the person is involved, suspected of involvement or attempted involvement in a crime and 2) the police officer believes that there are reasonable grounds for the arrest to be necessary.

3 For **detention**, think about the reasons for detention, time clocks, the role of the custody officer and the rights of the detainee.

4 For **interviews,** consider vulnerable detainees, the purpose of recorded information and the right to silence.

Below is an extract from one learner's response which outlines the grounds for a stop and search of Jamal, a client who was on his way home late at night carrying a heavy holdall.

Sample response extract

The police have the right to stop and search Jamal as stated in s.1 of PACE and code A provided the grounds for the search are that he is suspected of being in possession of prohibited articles such as stolen goods or offensive weapons. The search must take place in a public place and Jamal can only be required to remove outer clothing. The police officer must have reasonable grounds to suspect they will find prohibited articles, and the fact that it is late at night and Jamal has a heavy bag may suggest this. The police officer will use a standard procedure for the stop and search based on the name 'GOWISELY'. Jamal has cooperated with the officer and the use of reasonable force will not be required.

Sentence 2 points out where the search must take place.

Sentence 3 links the reason for the search to the facts.

Sentence 4 relates to procedure; the learner could have explained GOWISELY.

Now try this

Explain Jamal's rights if he were to be arrested and detained.

Answers

Unit 1: Dispute Solving in Civil Law

1. The features of civil law

Medical report on the injuries; police report; witness statements; statements of claimant or defendant

2. Civil court hierarchy

Jill would have to quantify the amount of damages she intends to claim based on her injuries and the damage to her vehicle. This would indicate the court in which she would issue her claim. As she has suffered serious injuries and she intends to claim damages in excess of £100,000 in total it is likely that the High Court would be used. She (or her lawyers) would prepare a claim form showing why she is entitled to damages and support this with medical reports and estimates for repairs to her car.

3. Role of judges in civil courts

The rule is a disincentive as the loser of an action could end up paying compensation to the winner, their own legal costs and the winner's legal costs. The rule means that only cases that have certain outcomes end up in court – and then usually only about the amount of compensation payable.

4. Negotiation and ombudsmen

- Contact installers and register complaint – initially orally, followed up in writing – letter or email.
- Negotiate resolution with installers.
- If unsuccessful, contact trade association asking to contact ombudsman.
- Send details of complaint to ombudsman in writing – keeping copies of all correspondence.
- Ombudsman decides dispute – if in favour of Asha, she should keep in contact with ombudsman to ensure installers follow the ombudsman's recommendation.

5. Arbitration

The clause in the contract will be binding on both parties. It means that instead of taking a dispute to court for a judge to settle, the dispute will be dealt with by an independent arbitrator, which is likely to be quicker and cheaper than using a court. The arbitrator can decide the case using written statements from both parties or call either or both to give oral evidence. The arbitrator's decision will be final and binding.

6. Conciliation and mediation

Similarities:
- both independent forms of dispute resolution
- the parties in dispute reach a resolution themselves.

Differences:
- the conciliator is more actively involved in helping to reach a solution
- the mediator attempts to keep a relationship together
- in conciliation, all parties discuss in same room; in mediation, parties are in separate rooms or buildings.

7. Alternative dispute resolution (ADR)

For:
- cheaper than court
- quicker than court
- less formal – no need for lawyers
- there are several methods that can be used

Against:
- outcome may be uncertain
- other party may be unwilling to use ADR
- may be difficulties enforcing award

8. Legal sources

1. Is there any legislation covering the relevant law? Is the legislation in force?
2. Is there any relevant delegated legislation – either bringing the primary legislation into force or filling in the gaps in the primary legislation?
3. Has the legislation been the subject of court cases interpreting the meaning of it?
4. If there is no legislation, is there a judicial precedent? If so, is the precedent from one of the higher appeal courts?
5. If there is no legislation or precedent, are there any articles in textbooks or journals that may help to explain the law?

9. Methods of appropriate professional communication

Client – misunderstands advice; prejudices case by acting inappropriately; discloses case details to affect outcome.
Court – judge may not accept arguments; judge may find against lawyer's client; case may be dismissed if inaccurate forms or papers are filed.

10. Solicitors' letters

Personal Injury Solicitors

Garden House
Kings Meadow
Brighton BN1
Tel 01632 960960

Email: pisolicitors@link.com
Website: www. pisolicitors

16 August 2017
Dear Sirs
We have not received a response from you or your clients, Image, to our letter of 8 August when we informed you that we were instructed by Julian Norris in relation to the injury suffered by him at your client's premises.

In our letter we informed you that we would be issuing a claim form on behalf of our client if we did not hear from you with an appropriate offer of compensation within 7 days of the date of our letter.

As nothing has been heard from you, and no offer of compensation made, we have issued a claim form in court, a copy of which is enclosed. The original has been sent directly to your clients.

Yours faithfully

Personal Injury Solicitors

To:
G. Brown & Co Solicitors
1 Seafront
Brighton

11. Brief to counsel

In the High Court of Justice
Queen's Bench Division

Case No 976 of 2017

BETWEEN

John Smith

v

ABC Recycling Co

BRIEF TO COUNSEL TO APPEAR IN COURT

Counsel will recall the initial instructions in this case to draft a statement of claim for the claimant who was injured at work.

This claim was issued in court and a defence has been issued by the employers denying the claim, alleging the injury was wholly caused by the claimant. Copies of the statement of claim and defence are attached.

Negotiations have been taking place for some time with the defendant's solicitors but at the time of writing, the defendants have not accepted their fault and they have not made any offer to settle the claim.

Instructing solicitors have therefore applied for a hearing date which has been set for 31 October 2017 at 10.30am. Counsel is requested to appear on behalf of the claimant at the court hearing and argue for a finding of liability and for special and general damages to be awarded to the claimant.

Personal Injury Solicitors
Garden House
Kings Meadow
Brighton BN1
Tel 01632 960960

12. Advice from solicitors and barristers

CAB – he could visit his local office for initial free advice. They are unlikely to be able to help if a formal claim needs to be issued.

Trade union – if he is a member of a union he could contact them for advice. It is likely they will give advice and their lawyers will deal with the whole case for him. He is unlikely to have to pay anything to the union.

Solicitor – he can go to a specialist personal injury solicitor but will have to pay privately or enter into a no win no fee arrangement and may have to take out before or after event insurance to cover costs of court action.

Barrister – he could go to a specialist barrister but will have to pay privately for their time.

13. Advice from Citizens Advice and Law Centres

- Check – is there a Citizens Advice office or Law Centre close by? Ideally they would want to see her.
- Is it an area of law that they deal with?
- Can they contact the other person on her behalf and negotiate a settlement?
- Will a fee be payable?
- Will she be referred on to a specialist lawyer or do they have specialists within the centre to take on the case?
- Will the case have to go to court?
- How long will the case take to reach a resolution?

14. Advice from insurance companies and online

Insurance: advantage – company will look after the interests of their insured; disadvantage – premium likely to be increased in future.

Internet: advantage – contact/support group could be set up; disadvantage – may not be able to find accurate advice/course of action.

15. Funding your own legal costs

Dear Javed,

I would advise you to go to a specialist personal injury solicitor for advice whether you have a claim. You will have to pay the solicitor privately for the time spent on your case or you could enter into a no win no fee arrangement with the solicitor. They will first assess the chance of success and if satisfied that you have a good chance of success will require you to take out insurance to cover costs of future court action. If you already have house or car insurance you may have 'before the event' cover, but you need to check the clauses in the policy. If you are not covered in this way you will have to pay a premium and take out 'after the event' cover which will pay out if you lose the case and costs are awarded against you.

Kind regards,
Nick

16. Funding by trade unions and the state

As Brian is a member of a union he should contact them for initial advice. It is likely that if they think he has a claim they will instruct their lawyers, who will deal with the whole case for him. He is unlikely to have to pay anything to the union or the lawyers and any compensation received will be wholly his.

17. Costs in taking legal action

(a) The court fee to make a claim for £10,000 is £455 for a paper form and £410 for an online claim.

(b) The court fee to make a claim for £100,000 is 5% of the claim for a paper form (£5000) and 4.5% of the claim for an online claim (£4500).

18. The doctrine of precedent in court hierarchy

The *ratio decidendi* is 'all dogs must be controlled when on the street'. This is *ratio decidendi* because the case involves (a material fact) an uncontrolled dog biting someone.

The *obiter dicta* is 'I do not think this would apply to a cat or a rabbit.' This is *obiter dicta* as the case does not involve any other animals. This gives a strong hint to judges and lawyers that this particular bit of law only applies to dogs. Therefore, a case with an uncontrolled cat biting someone would not make the owner of the cat liable for failure to control the animal.

19. The hierarchy of the courts

The Supreme Court must follow its previous decisions except where the 1966 Practice Statement can be applied. Here the court may 'Depart from its previous decisions when it appears right to do so'.

The Court of Appeal must follow its previous decisions except when the law in **Young v Bristol Aeroplane Co 1944** can be applied. This allows the Court to avoid its binding precedent in three circumstances:

- there are two conflicting decisions of the Court of Appeal
- the decision of the Court of Appeal conflicts with a later Supreme Court decision
- the Court of Appeal decision was decided *per incuriam*.

20. *Ratio decidendi* and *obiter dicta*

1 The person giving the information was an A&E receptionist; in previous cases, the persons giving information had been ambulance service telephonists.

2 *Ratio decidendi*.

3 The hospital's duty not to misinform patients was not removed 'by interposing non-medical reception staff as a first point of contact'. *Obiter dicta* it was said that although there is no duty on receptionists to give wider advice or information, they were under a duty not to provide misinformation.

21. Law reporting

The law report follows the sequence of:
* headings with data including the court
* the judges
* the case name
* the dates the case was heard
* the date the judgment was delivered
* the reference for the law report.

Each judge's reasoned decision is then set out exactly as the judge stated it.

The law report usually sets out the facts of the case, the history of the appeals and the relevant law.

The judge then may comment on the law and sometimes makes distinctions between the present case and the existing law or points out how the law is to be refined.

The law is then applied to the facts and a decision made.

This continues for each judge in appeal cases where there is more than one judge.

At the end, the names of the firms of solicitors for the parties to the case are listed and the initials or names of the barrister authorising the law report as a valid transcript of what was said in court.

22. Following precedent

1 The precedent set can be used to defeat his claim as a lamp post can be seen as similar to a road sign as street furniture. This means no duty of care is owed.

2 An appeal could be successful if the appeal reached the Supreme Court or the precedent could be shown to have fallen within one of the three exceptions in **Young v Bristol Aeroplace Co 1944**.

23. Avoiding binding precedents

Mr and Mrs Balfour were living happily together. They made an agreement about payment of a regular sum to Mrs Balfour while her husband worked abroad. This agreement was not legally enforceable as it was a purely domestic arrangement. **Merritt v Merritt 1970** could be distinguished as the husband and wife were separated when they made the agreement about payment of a regular sum so this was seen as intended to be legally binding.

24. Researching and interpreting case law

25. Advantages and disadvantages of the doctrine of precedent

1. These cases might form precedents as they are all related to road traffic accidents involving hitting another vehicle.

2. It could be different as a motor racing circuit is on private land and all the participants realise there are dangers involved. These dangers are accepted by participants providing the circuit is maintained and run in accordance with nationally set standards by the motor racing governing body.

26. Duty of care: proximity

Arguments for proximity:
* She heard the crash.
* She is related to the victim – **McLoughlin v O'Brian 1983**.

Arguments against proximity:
* She was in a safe place at the time of the crash – **Bourhill v Young 1943**.
* The relationship may not be close enough.

27. Duty of care: foreseeability

Naseem
This is foreseeable to the reasonable person as fence posts falling out of a truck will damage anything they hit or are hit by.

Anthony
This is also foreseeable as it is likely all sorts of road users will pass by in the time following the incident.

28. Duty of care: fair, just and reasonable

Example
The facts and decision of your chosen cases(s) could be written as follows:

Case: **Michael v Chief Constable of South Wales 2015**

Facts: The claimants were the parents and children of Joanna Michael, who had been murdered by her former partner. She made a 999 call in which she explained that her ex-boyfriend had come to her house and found her with another man and told her he was going to kill her. The call handler said she did not hear her mention this threat to kill, and the call was graded as only requiring a response within 60 minutes. About 14 minutes later, Joanna Michael called 999 again, she screamed and the line went dead. The police got there 8 minutes later but unfortunately found that she had been stabbed to death by her ex-partner.

Decision: The test for the existence of the duty of care permits judges to impose a duty or not according to their perceptions of what public policy requires. In this case they thought there should be no duty of care owed by the police.

29. The objective standard

You need to start a list. Go through other areas you have studied for Applied Law and then add in examples under 'objective tests: the reasonable person'.

Have a second list for areas of law where the subjective test is used. You will find some in Unit 3 of Applied Law.

30. The reasonable person test

Bolam v Friern Hospital Management Committee 1957
The duty had not been breached because the doctor reached the standard required by medical opinion. The fact that there were differing opinions meant that the reasonable doctor would follow whichever opinion they thought correct.

Nettleship v Weston 1971
The standard of care expected of a learner driver is that of the reasonably competent driver. This is because the law balances the interests of claimant and defendant. Also, car insurance is compulsory.

Mullin v Richards 1998
She was found not to be in breach of duty. She was only expected to meet the standard of a reasonable 15-year-old, not that of a reasonable adult. Children are judged by the standard of the reasonable person of that age, so the test is still objective.

31. Risk factors and breach of duty 1

Bolton v Stone 1951
The greater the risk, the more care must be taken if there is not to be a breach of duty: here the risk was very low and the reasonable person would not think precautions were necessary to prevent the risk.

32. Risk factors and breach of duty 2

Latimer v AEC 1953

The defendant only had to take reasonable precautions to minimise the risk and they had done so in this case. The reasonable person would only have done what AEC did as shutting the factory would have been excessively cautious.

33. Factual causation

Mohammed's employer is the factual cause of the broken leg and the other injuries in the crash as if he had not been negligent the broken leg would not have happened. With respect to the other injuries, there is a new act intervening, the crash, which breaks the chain of causation between the employer and the other injuries.

34. Remoteness of damage

This is based on the case of **Hughes v Lord Advocate 1963**. When an accident is of a different type and kind from anything that a reasonable person could have foreseen, he is not liable for it. But if it is only an extreme form of a foreseeable injury he will be liable. Some injury by burning from the lamp can be foreseen, and the explosion is just an extreme form of this.

35. Awarding damages and mitigating loss

1 General – not easily quantified.
2 Special – quantified.
3 Special if fees occurred before the date of the trial as they will be quantified. Fees after that will be general as they are not easily quantifiable.
4 Special – quantified.
5 General – not easily quantified.

36. Damages

Deafness – the award depends on the level of disability and whether it is combined with speech loss. So for partial hearing loss, the award is likely to be in the area of £5000 to £30,000 and this overlaps with loss of hearing in one ear.

Impotence – here compensation is heavily dependent on the age of the claimant. The award of damages is balanced between male impotence and female sterility. The amount can reach £100,000.

Bowels and Bladder – each of these can reach nearly £100,000. This reflects the effect such injury can have on leading life without the disability.

37. Contributory negligence

In **Smith v Finch 2009** it was argued that a deduction of 15% for failing to wear a cycle helmet should be made in a case involving a cyclist who had sustained a serious brain injury following a collision with a motorcyclist, further to the guidance provided by the Highway Code and the observations of Lord Denning in the precedent in **Froom v Butcher 1975**. The problem is whether there is evidence as to whether the helmet would have prevented or lessened the injury. Here, contributory fault failed as the claimant's head had struck the ground at more than 12mph, the speed at which cycling helmets ceased, at the time, to be an effective form of protective headgear.

38. How damages are paid

1 With such a long life expectancy, there would be a danger that a lump sum, even invested very effectively, might prove insufficient in later years.
2 The lump sum would be exceedingly large and managing the money would be an additional burden on the presumed carers, his parents.

39. The burden of proof and *res ipsa loquitur*

1 The thing that caused the damage was under the sole control of the defendant – the surgeon (and his team) were solely in control of the swab.
2 The incident is one that would not have happened unless someone had been negligent – swabs do not normally get left inside bodies.
3 There is no other obvious reason as to why the incident occurred – this is self-evident.

40. Your Unit 1 set task

Answers will vary dependent on the latest Sample Assessment Material.

41. Research and making notes

In **Hill v Chief Constable of West Yorkshire 1988**, the mother of Yorkshire Ripper's last victim sued the police for failing to catch her daughter's killer.

Legal principle – it was not fair, just and reasonable for the police to owe duty of care to ordinary member of public not known to them.

42. Outlining and applying

1 Refer back to meeting.
2 Purpose of damages in tort.
3 Outline two forms of damages in tort – special damages and general damages – and when they can each be claimed.
4 Outline next steps – obtain evidence to support claim.

43. Explaining and analysing

In the case of **Wells v Cooper 1958** the Court of Appeal decided that the level of care and skill required of a householder carrying out his own repairs was to be judged according to the degree of care and skill that a reasonably skilled amateur carpenter might be expected to apply to the work in question. This was not as high a standard as if the work was carried out by a professional. In this case, the degree of care and skill required is that of a reasonably competent driver driving on the same road. As the defendant was speeding, this was not at the standard of a reasonably competent driver and so he has broken his duty of care.

44. Evaluating

Mr Paris was clearly owed a duty of care by his employers as he was doing his job in the workplace. He was carrying out a risky job as a welder and he should have been given some protective clothes and eye guards.

His employers were aware that he had suffered a previous accident and that he only had one good eye and that if this eye was damaged by an accident he would have been completely blinded. So he was more vulnerable than the other workers. It is the failure of his employers to provide him with protection that led directly to his injury.

On the other hand, the employers could argue that he caused or contributed to the accident and his injury. However, the evidence from his supervisor and fellow employees does not support this claim.

It seems that Mr Paris has a strong claim against his employers and should pursue them for compensation as he is unlikely to be able to find work again.

45. Presentations

After a duty of care is established, the second test for proving negligence is that the duty has been broken.

- Defendants are judged according to the reasonable person test – did the defendant fail to do something that the reasonable person would do or do something the reasonable person would not do?
- Professionals are judged according to the standard of others in the same profession (**Bolam v Friern Hospital Management Committee 1957**).
- Learners are judged according to the standard of the competent (**Nettleship v Weston 1971**).
- Children are judged according to the standard of other children of the same age (**Mullin v Richards 1998**).
- No breach of duty by Richards as she was judged according to what other 15-year-olds would do.

46. Writing solicitors' letters

Dear Mrs Orchard,

Following your telephone call today, I confirm that my firm will be pleased to act for you in making a claim for compensation as a result of the injuries you suffered in your recent unfortunate accident.

In order that I can proceed with your claim, please write a detailed account of how and when the accident happened, including the name of the boy who injured you. Please also give me the full name and address of your employer as I understand the accident happened at your place of work.

I understand from you that you were taken to hospital after the accident and are now under the care of your doctor. I will need to know the name and address of your doctor and which hospital you were treated at. I will also need your written consent to obtain your medical reports.

I can confirm that my firm will be acting on a 'no win, no fee' basis for you so that the fees will be recovered from the defendant when we are successful. I understand you have a house insurance policy that can act as a 'before the event' policy so I do not need to ask you for any monies now.

I look forward to receiving your statement. If there is anything at all during the case that you do not understand or wish to discuss, please do not hesitate to contact me.

Yours sincerely

Alison Agnew
Solicitor

47. Case file notes

Outline the case
- Provide an outline of the case history
- Details of the person they will be representing
- When and where they will be required to represent them

Explain relevant case documents
- Witness statements
- Medical reports
- Confirmation of loss of earnings

Suggest the next steps
- Outline the argument for negligence and duty of care.
- Outline the argument for damages for pain and suffering, loss of amenity, and loss of earnings.

Unit 3: Applying the Law

48. *Actus reus* – criminal actions and conduct

Actus reus means guilty act and is one element that is used to establish criminal liability. Some examples of *actus reus* for murder are: shooting, stabbing and strangling.

For each *actus reus*, evidence would be produced linking the defendant to the *actus reus*, which is the cause of death. For example – fingerprints on a weapon, DNA or blood on the defendant's clothes, or possessions matching the victim.

49. *Mens rea* – intention

The hitman: His aim is to make money by agreeing to kill the business partner – this is the motive. He intends to kill her so that payment will be made – the intention is the *mens rea*.

The man hiring the hitman: We do not know why he wants his business partner to be killed but he shows that by planning the attack he intends the killing. He will not carry out the *actus reus*. A crime needs both *actus reus* and *mens rea*.

The hitman will be charged with murder and the man will be charged with conspiracy to murder.

50. Criticism and reform of current law

Changes to the law may be needed because:
- The law is old fashioned and out of date, such as a definition from 1797 for murder.
- Advances in technology can lead to the need for the law to change. For example, social media sites being used to threaten, bully and harass people.
- It may be necessary to simplify the law so that it is easier to be applied to cases in courts. This can increase access to justice. Introducing the Corporate Manslaughter and Corporate Homicide Act 2007 has led to an increase in convictions.

51. Voluntary manslaughter as a partial defence to murder

Mitigating factors:
- The age of the defendant. A child under 10 cannot be criminally liable. For a defendant aged under 18 and found guilty of murder, the starting point is 12 years for the minimum tariff. For those over 21 the starting point can be between 15 and 30 years depending on the circumstances.
- A lack of premeditation. This could include instances where the defendant lost control due to provocation.
- A belief by the defendant that the murder was an act of mercy. For example, assisting the death of a terminally ill person.

52. Loss of control

Impact of the Coroners and Justice Act 2009

Before 2009	From 2009
Provocation defined as a sudden and temporary loss of control by things said, done or both. Subjective and objective test.	Loss of control need not be sudden or temporary. Subjective and objective tests. Triggered by fear of violence or things done or said giving the defendant a sense of being seriously wronged.
Diminished responsibility – abnormality of mind to impair responsibility for acts and omissions. The abnormality could arise from disease, injury or impaired intellectual functioning and lead to a wide range of physical and psychological conditions being accepted.	Abnormality of mental functioning caused by a recognised medical condition and substantially affecting understanding, forming rational judgement or exercising self-control.

53. Diminished responsibility

Loss of control s.54 and s.55 Coroners and Justice Act 2009 ▷

1. Defendant lost control.
2. There was a qualifying trigger.
3. A person of the same age and sex and with a normal degree of tolerance might have reacted in the same way in the circumstances. ▷

QUALIFYING TRIGGERS
1. Fear of serious violence from the victim to the defendant or another, or 2. Things said or done or both forming circumstances of an extremely grave nature and that caused the defendant to have a justifiable sense of being seriously wronged.

Loss of control s.52 Coroners and Justice Act 2009 ▷

Defendant had an abnormality of mental functioning. ▷

Resulted from a recognised medical condition which substantially impaired the defendants' ability to understand the nature of their conduct, or form a rational judgement, or exercise self-control.

54. Reform

Headline 1: The motive of the defendant was to steal the victim's money to pay a gambling debt. This suggests that the defendant had thought about his actions and had planned the attack. The *mens rea* of direct intent may be established. This is where the defendant's aim and objective was to carry out the killing and at the time of the killing, he had the *mens rea* of intent. If this is established, the likely verdict would be guilty of murder and a mandatory life sentence would be imposed.

Headline 2: This relates to another fatal attack, which is an unlawful homicide. However, the defendant claimed that he was instructed to commit the killings by aliens. Such a statement suggests there may be a mental health issue. If the defendant is classed as insane before the trial, he may not be fit to plead, or if he was found to be insane at the time of the killings he would be found not guilty by reason of insanity. This is known as a special verdict and the judge has three options:
1. Imposing a hospital order
2. Imposing a supervision order
3. Releasing the defendant.

Another alternative is that the defence may raise the partial defence of loss of control from s.52 of the Coroners and Justice Act 2009. If it is accepted that the *mens rea* of the defendant was affected by a recognised medical condition, which led to an abnormality of mental functioning that substantially impaired his ability to understand the nature of his actions, form a rational judgement or exercise self-control, this is a partial defence. The effect of a partial defence is to reduce a murder charge to a charge of voluntary manslaughter.

55. Voluntary and involuntary manslaughter

Scenario 1: A doctor who was in charge of the anaesthetic in an operation failed to notice that a tube had fallen from the patient's mouth and that the patient was being starved of oxygen. The patient died. This scenario is similar to the case of **R v Adomako 1994** where the doctor was charged with gross negligence manslaughter. The offence requires:
• A duty of care – the doctor has a duty to care for all patients.
• A breach of duty – the doctor was not doing his job properly; he should have been watching the patient all the time and making sure that the patient had oxygen.

• The breach of duty caused death – in this case the patient would not have died had the doctor taken care so factual and legal causation can be proved.
• The carelessness is so bad that it can be classed as criminal – in this scenario the jury would decide that the negligence is 'gross'.
• The case falls into the category of involuntary manslaughter by means of gross negligence.

Scenario 2: In the middle of the night a burglar broke into a cottage but was disturbed by the householder who was a 90-year-old man. The burglar pushed the old man to the ground and kicked his head before running away. The old man had been healthy but frail and died two days later in hospital. This is a case of unlawful act manslaughter, sometimes called constructive manslaughter. The following must be proved:
• The defendant committed an intentional act (*mens rea*) – in this case he kicked the old man.
• The act committed was criminally unlawful – in this case the burglary was unlawful but also the defendant hurt the old man, which could be classed as assault and battery, ABH or GBH depending on the injuries sustained by the old man.
• The act committed was dangerous – in this case it was more dangerous as the victim was a frail old man.
• The act committed caused death – there is a direct link between the burglar kicking the old man and his death, so factual and legal causation can be established.

The defendant has committed involuntary manslaughter by means of an unlawful act. Involuntary manslaughter is where the defendant did not intend to cause death but was reckless.

56. Unlawful act manslaughter

Two men broke into a house. They found the car keys for a car parked outside but they were disturbed by the householder. They then fatally attacked the householder while he was trying to protect his car and property.
• Breaking into the house is burglary, which requires entering a building as a trespasser with an intent to steal or inflict grievous bodily harm. The two men were trespassers and intended to steal, showing *actus reus* and *mens rea*.
• Taking the car keys is theft which is classed as dishonest appropriation of property belonging to another with an intent to permanently deprive the owner of it. The two men wanted not only the keys but also the car.
• Attacking the householder, the charge would depend on the injuries – it could be assault and battery, ABH or GBH. In this case the attack was fatal so the *actus reus* is causing death and the *mens rea* is recklessness as the two men did not intend to kill.
• If the two men caused the death of the householder and there was no intervening act to break the chain of causation, the charge would be unlawful act manslaughter and the prosecution would have to establish the elements – a deliberate and dangerous act was committed, the act was criminally unlawful and finally that the act caused death.

57. Gross negligence manslaughter

Indictable offences are serious offences that are tried in the Crown Court. If a defendant pleads not guilty to the charges a trial takes place where prosecution and defence barristers present the case. A jury consisting of 12 people, chosen at random, decide on the verdict. If it is a guilty verdict, the judge passes sentence. Murder carries a mandatory life sentence. The judge has no other option and will declare a life sentence but will set a minimum term to be spent in prison. For an adult this can range from 15 to 30 years before release can be considered. Once released, the defendant is still on licence for the rest of their life. This means that if they commit further offences they go straight back to prison. An exception is where a judge passes a whole life term, which means that the defendant will never be released.

For all cases other than murder, the judge passes a discretionary sentence. This means that the judge has some leeway in passing sentence depending on the facts and circumstances of the case and the defendant. The judge will however follow sentencing guidelines produced by the Sentencing Council. The purpose of a sentence is:

* to punish the offender
* to reduce crime
* to reform and rehabilitate the offender
* to protect the public
* to make the offender give something back – restorative justice.

58. Corporate manslaughter

An employer could be responsible for the death of an employee, a client, visitor or a member of the public by being grossly negligent. Three examples of such negligence are:

1   Failing to provide proper training, supervision and safety equipment. In each example, the employer has committed an omission – a failure to do something that a reasonably prudent employer would do. These types of behaviour were the cause of death of Steven Berry in the case of **R v Lion Steel Ltd 2012** where the company was fined £480,000.
2   Failing to maintain equipment such as machinery, lifts or vehicles. This occurred in the case of **R v Baldwins Crane Hire Ltd 2015**. A vehicle had faulty brakes, which led to an accident where the driver, an employee, died.
3   Failing to make sensible management decisions taking into account health and safety. This was the case in **R v Sherwood Rise Ltd 2016**. The company was found guilty of corporate manslaughter: the care home failed to show adequate care, nutrition, accommodation and support for an elderly resident who died weighing just 3 stone 12 pounds.

59. Corporate Manslaughter and Corporate Homicide Act 2007 – elements required

Penalties for corporate manslaughter include unlimited fines, remedial and publicity orders.

	Pros	Cons
Unlimited fines	Higher fines can make the victim's family feel that justice has been done. Higher fines can act as a warning to other companies.	Some critics think that the only appropriate sentence would be prison. A high fine could cause insolvency for the company and redundancies for the workers.
Remedial order	This orders the company to put the defect right that caused the death. This protects employees in the future.	The victim's family will think that this action has come too late and that health and safety should be proactive and not reactive.
Publicity order	This can warn others that the defendant company did not follow health and safety.	It can deter investors, customers and clients.

60. Theft and *actus reus*

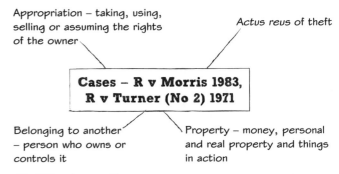

Appropriation – taking, using, selling or assuming the rights of the owner

Actus reus of theft

Cases – R v Morris 1983, R v Turner (No 2) 1971

Belonging to another – person who owns or controls it

Property – money, personal and real property and things in action

61. Theft and *mens rea*

The *actus reus* is the appropriation of property belonging to another.

Shoplifting is the taking goods from a store without paying. The shoplifter takes the items, which is an appropriation of property, the goods at that point belong to the store. Ownership of the goods passes to a customer only when the goods are paid for. Pickpocketing amounts to theft as a person secretly takes items from another person – this is an appropriation. The property is usually purses, wallets or mobile phones.

The *mens rea* is dishonesty and an intention to permanently deprive the owner.

The shoplifter is dishonest as they have no intention of paying for the goods or returning them to the owner.

The pickpocket is dishonest as the perpetrator knows the property belongs to another person and there is no intention to return the property to the owner.

62. Robbery 1

Mitigating factors include: opportunism, voluntary return of property, age of offender, peer pressure, immaturity of offender, first offence of violence, remorse, cooperation with police.
Mitigating factors can influence the judge to make a more lenient sentencing decision as the defendant is seen as less blameworthy.

63. Robbery 2

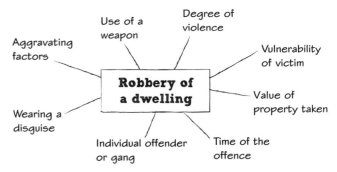

Aggravating factors

Use of a weapon

Degree of violence

Vulnerability of victim

Robbery of a dwelling

Value of property taken

Wearing a disguise

Individual offender or gang

Time of the offence

64. The two types of burglary

Section 9(1)(a) A person is guilty of burglary if they enter any building or part of a building as a trespasser with intent to steal or to inflict GBH or to do unlawful damage.

Section 9(1)(b) A person is guilty of burglary if, having entered any building or part of a building, they steal or attempt to steal, or inflict or attempt to inflict grievous bodily harm.

The Hatton Gardens heist satisfies both definitions.

The gang entered the building as trespassers – they used heavy cutting gear to break into Hatton Gardens Safe Deposit Ltd. They intended to steal the jewellery held there and they also caused criminal damage to the building. s.9(1)(b)

The gang did enter the building and did steal £14 million pounds worth of jewels, which they removed in holdalls and wheelie bins. s.9(1)(a)

65. Liability for burglary

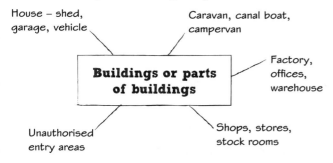

House – shed, garage, vehicle

Caravan, canal boat, campervan

Buildings or parts of buildings

Factory, offices, warehouse

Unauthorised entry areas

Shops, stores, stock rooms

66. Fraud by false representation – *actus reus*

Cybercrime covers offences committed via the internet or aided by computer technology.

1. Ransomware – computers are hacked and locked until the owner pays a ransom. The *actus reus* is hacking into and disabling the system and demanding money.
2. Dating scam – befriending victims online before demanding money or bank details. The *actus reus* is making false representations to the victims.
3. Online shopping scams – people buying and paying for non-existent goods and services. The *actus reus* is making a false representation that the site is legitimate and the goods and services are available.

67. Fraud by false representation – *mens rea*

The *actus reus* is making a false representation which is untrue or misleading. The woman claimed as a single parent but in fact lived with her partner.

The *mens rea* is the knowledge that the statement is untrue or misleading and dishonesty.

The woman knew she was living with her partner and that the statement about being a single parent was untrue. She was dishonest and intended to make a gain as she knew that she was not entitled to the benefits being claimed.

68. Criminal damage

Section 1(1): A person who without lawful excuse destroys or damages any property belonging to another intending to destroy or damage any such property or being reckless as to whether any such property would be destroyed or damaged shall be guilty of an offence.

Ann has broken the window intentionally to gain entrance to the house and has committed damage. However, it would not be criminal damage as she had a lawful excuse for breaking the window. Her landlord would have consented to her actions. This is a lawful excuse as outlined in s.5. The defendant believed that the owner had, or would have, consented to it if he had known or the defendant destroyed, damaged or threatened to do it in order to protect property belonging to himself or another.

69. Arson

Section 1(3) of the Criminal Damage Act 1971 creates the offence of arson, which is defined as destroying or damaging property by fire.

The offence of aggravated arson in s.1(4) also requires a *mens rea* element relating to endangering life.

Derek set fire to his nightclub. He owns the club along with a silent partner. His motive is to claim the insurance money. He has committed the *actus reus* as he has destroyed the property by fire. The *mens rea* of intention to destroy or recklessness can also be established. Derek would be charged with s.1(3) and s.1(4) as he was aware that the cleaners were inside the building and he put their lives at risk. Derek could face a maximum sentence of life for arson.

70. Duress by threats

Duress as a complete defence	Partial defences
Available for most offences except murder and attempted murder.	Available only for a murder charge.
If successfully pleaded leads to an acquittal.	If successfully pleaded it reduces the charge to voluntary manslaughter, meaning that the sentence will be discretionary.
There are two types – duress by threats and duress of circumstances. The defendant's actions are influenced by fear.	Loss of control must be established and the qualifying triggers satisfied.

71. Duress by circumstances

Duress by threats	Duress by circumstance
Fear caused by threats and accompanied with an instruction to commit a crime.	Fear caused by circumstances causing the defendant to fear death or serious injury.

Two-stage test from **R v Graham 1982**:
1. The defendant must reasonably believe and have good cause to fear the threat made or arising through the circumstances.
2. A sober person of reasonable firmness sharing the defendant's characteristics would have acted in the same way.
Must not be self-induced.
Threat must be directed at the defendant, a member of their immediate family or someone close relying on the defendant for their own safety.
The jury must consider the reasonableness of the defendant's perceptions and conduct.
There must be no evasive action against the threat the defendant could have taken.

72. Intoxication

Andre has become voluntarily intoxicated. The intoxication will only be relevant if Andre lacks *mens rea*, which for murder is intention. However, Andre formed the required *mens rea* before he became intoxicated.

Murder is a crime of specific intent and in a crime of specific intent if the defendant has not formed *mens rea* the charge can be reduced to a lesser charge such as manslaughter. This occurred in **R v Lipman 1970**.

Andre's voluntary intoxication did not affect the *mens rea* – it was Dutch courage and he would be found guilty for murder and subject to a mandatory life sentence.

73. Self-defence

Common law defence	Statutory defence
Formed through precedent from previous cases	Defined in the Criminal Law Act 1967
A person can use force against violent assaults to defend themselves, another or their property.	A person can use force against the commission of any crime to defend themselves, another or their property.

For both defences, there are two key questions:
- Given the circumstances, was the use of force necessary?
- Was the amount of force used reasonable?

Limitations	
Can only be used to protect against violent assaults.	An actual crime must be being committed.
Interpretation of necessary and reasonable can be problematic.	Interpretation of necessary and reasonable can be problematic.

74. Insanity and automatism

For sane automatism two things must be proved:
1 The defendant suffered a total loss of voluntary control which was not self-induced.
2 The action was caused by an external factor.

An example of self-induced automatism could be: drinking alcohol when taking prescribed medication against medical advice.

75. Stop and search

Examples include:
- searching for drugs
- searching for stolen property
- searching for weapons.

The police officer needs to have reasonable grounds for a stop and search. If not, their actions would go against the codes of practice and could be classed as assault. The officer also needs to follow proper procedure, such as informing the suspect of the reason for the search. If the police officer discovers illegal possession the suspect will be cautioned, arrested, detained and interviewed. The suspect may then be charged or released depending on the investigation.

76. Arrest

Reasons for arresting a person include:
- where the name and address of the person cannot be ascertained
- to prevent injury to that person or another or to prevent loss of or damage to property
- to prevent an offence of public indecency or obstruction of the highway
- to protect a child or vulnerable person
- to allow for a prompt and effective investigation of a crime
- to prevent the prosecution of the case from being risked.

Reasonable suspicion is used to prevent arrests being based on personal factors or discrimination. Reasonable suspicion limits the powers of the police and helps to strike a balance between law-abiding people freely going about their business and the need for the police to investigate crime.

77. Detention

The right to legal advice and the right to a phone call may be delayed in limited circumstances.
1 If it would lead to interference with evidence connected to an indictable offence.
2 If it would lead to interference or injury to another person.
3 If it would alert other people suspected of having committed such an offence but who have not yet been arrested.
4 If it would lead to problems in the recovery of any property obtained as a result of such an offence.

78. Interviews at the police station

Tape recorded interviews provide:
- accurate and timely evidence to be used in court and the tapes are sealed so that they cannot be tampered with before the trial takes place
- evidence that the investigating officers were carrying out the interview appropriately and not using oppression to force a confession
- evidence that the accused person was capable of being interviewed, of listening and understanding.

79. Searches and samples

Forensic science is the application of scientific knowledge and methods to legal problems and criminal investigations to provide objective and logical evidence for a court of law. Forensics are constantly making advances as technology develops. This can lead to more reliable evidence such as DNA analysis, computer reconstructions and mobile phone technology. The more reliable the evidence is, miscarriages of justice are less likely.

80. Your Unit 3 set task

Answers will vary dependent on the latest Sample Assessment Material.

81. Reading task information

'Body found in Wheelie Bin'
- Murder and voluntary manslaughter
- *Actus reus*, *mens rea* and causation
- Loss of control
- Intoxication
- Court proceedings
- Sentencing
- Supporting case law, statute and statistics

'Mission Impossible'
- Theft and burglary
- *Actus reus* and *mens rea* elements
- Arrest and detention
- Court proceedings
- Sentencing
- Supporting case law, statute and statistics

82. Researching fatal offences

Legal definition of insanity: the definition comes from the case of **Daniel M'Naghten 1843** who was accused of murder and acquitted on grounds of insanity. The decision was controversial and a panel of judges reviewed the law relating to insanity and came up with the following rules:
- The defendant is presumed to be sane unless the contrary is proved.
- It must be proved that at the time of committing the act the defendant was labouring under a defect of reason, from disease of the mind so as not to know the nature and quality of the act he was doing or, if he did know, that he did not know that what he was doing was wrong.

The elements to be proved are:
- a defect of reasoning, which means the defendant's ability to use the power of reasoning must be impaired
- disease of the mind – this must cause the impairment and the origin of the disease of the mind can be physical or mental
- not knowing what they are doing – the defendant must not know what they are physically doing and what the consequences of their actions would be, and
- not knowing what they are doing is wrong – the defendant must not know that their actions are wrong or illegal.

83. Researching property offences

Legal definition of theft: theft is defined in s.1 of the Theft Act 1968 as follows: 'A person is guilty of theft if he dishonestly appropriates property belonging to another with the intention of permanently depriving the other of it.'

Actus reus:
- Appropriating
- Property
- Belonging to another

Mens rea:
- Dishonesty
- Intention to permanently deprive the other

84. Making notes

1. Explain legal terminology to a client:

Murder – this offence is the intentional killing of another person. The defendant must cause the death of the person and mean to do it or act in a way that is virtually certain to cause death or serious injury. The judge has to give a life sentence if a defendant is found guilty of murder.

Voluntary manslaughter – this is exactly the same as murder but there are factors that mean the charge can be reduced to manslaughter. The reasons for a charge to be reduced are that the defendant lost control through fear or as a result of an abnormality of mental functioning related to a recognised medical condition. The effect of such a charge is that if the defendant is found to be guilty the judge can choose the sentence, which can range from a suspended sentence up to a life sentence.

Actus reus – for most crimes including fatal offences, two parts have to be proved. The first is *actus reus*; this is a Latin term that means the prohibited act. The *actus reus* is an action (such as stabbing) or a failure to act (such as starving a young child) that causes death.

Mens rea – this is an essential element of a crime. It is a Latin term that means guilty mind and it has to be proved alongside the *actus reus*. It means that, for murder, the defendant at the time of the killing intended to cause death or grievous bodily harm.

Causation – this is another element that has to be proved. There must be a link between what the defendant did and the death. It is also called the chain of causation and for criminal liability the chain of causation must not be broken by an intervening event; for example, if the defendant stabs a victim but the hospital treatment is wholly inappropriate and grossly negligent, the treatment could become the cause of death.

2. Duress by threat:
- This does not apply to murder or attempted murder.
- The threat must be of death or serious injury.
- 2-stage Graham test – subjective and objective strands.
- Threats must be directly linked to criminal conduct.
- The threat cannot be self-induced.
- There must have been no evasive action open to the defendant.
- Cases – **Valderamma Vega 1985**

85. Reviewing further information: fatal offences

Loss of control is a partial defence that can reduce a murder charge to voluntary manslaughter (s.54 CJA 2009). There must be a qualifying trigger, which could be fear of serious violence or caused by things said, done or both making the defendant feel a sense of being seriously wronged. There is no evidence of an argument where allegations could have been made to make Mr Kennedy lose control and a further requirement of the defence is that such things said or done must be such as to make a person of the same sex and age and with a normal degree of tolerance and self-restraint react in the same or a similar way to the defendant. Sexual infidelity alone cannot be a qualifying trigger as illustrated in **R v Clinton 2012**. It is unlikely that Mr Kennedy could rely on s.54 as a partial defence. However, s.52 of the CJA 2009 could apply provided Mr Kennedy's actions were based on mental impairment related to a recognised medical condition rather than just jealousy. It would have to be proved that his ability to:
- understand the nature of his conduct
- form a rational judgement, and
- exercise self-control

was substantially impaired and provided an explanation for Mr Kennedy's acts in committing the killing.

86. Structuring a report

Introduction
Murder – legal definition, *actus reus*, *mens rea*, causation
Voluntary manslaughter – loss of control and mitigating factors (CJA 2009)
Insanity as a potential claim by the defence
Intoxication – voluntary, involuntary, specific and basic intent offences
Conclusion including consequences and likely outcomes

87. Using your plan to write a report

Conclusion
Mr Kennedy would face trial at a Crown Court as the offence he is charged with is an indictable offence. The jury consisting of 12 people selected at random from the electoral roll would reach a verdict and the judge would be responsible for the sentencing. Mr Kennedy's claims of a partial or complete defence have been unsuccessful as there is no evidence that he satisfied the qualifying triggers for loss of control. In relation to mental impairment the jury have not accepted medical evidence of a recognised medical condition and have related his behaviour to pure jealousy. In terms of intoxication, Mr Kennedy's state was self-induced as it was voluntary intoxication and in itself this shows recklessness. However, murder is an offence of specific intent and recklessness alone will not suffice. Voluntary intoxication can only reduce a charge of murder to manslaughter if the defendant was not capable of forming the required *mens rea* – intent to kill or cause grievous bodily harm. The jury have decided that the prosecution have established the *actus reus* and *mens rea* beyond reasonable doubt. The consequence for Mr Kennedy is that he will face a mandatory life sentence and the judge will set a minimum term to be spent in prison before he can be released on licence. The starting points for life sentences for murder are set out in the Criminal Justice Act 2003 (as amended) and the starting point for a murder committed with a knife or other weapon is 25 years, although the judge will also take into account aggravating and mitigating factors.

88. Writing a report: appropriate terminology

Answers will vary dependent on case chosen.

89. Reviewing further information: property offences

Theft

The *actus reus* consists of:

Appropriation of property, this means using the property as if you are the owner though it does not belong to you, for example, selling, using, keeping or lending. Appropriation is defined in s.3 of the Theft Act. In the case of **R v Morris 1983**, altering price labels was classed as appropriation as only the owner of the goods had a right to do this.

Property is defined in s.4 as money, personal property, real property, things in action and other intangible property.

Section 5 deals with the fact that the property must belong to another – this means the person who owns or controls the property.

In conjunction with the *actus reus*, the *mens rea* has to be established.

Dishonesty is part of the *mens rea* and in s.2 of the Theft Act examples are provided when a person's actions would not be classed as dishonest – if they believed the owner would give consent, if they believed they had a legal right to the goods or if the defendant believed the true owner could not be found by taking reasonable steps. Dishonesty is a difficult concept to establish and the courts use a two-stage test from the case of **R v Ghosh 1982**.

- Were the actions of the defendant dishonest by the standards of reasonable and honest people? And if so
- Did the defendant know it was dishonest by those standards? The second part of the *mens rea* is intention to deprive the other of it. This means the defendant treats the property as his own regardless of the rights of the owner as in **R v Lavender 1994**.

90. Writing case file notes

Description

Give an account in words of someone or something, including all of the relevant characteristics, qualities or events. Give an account of something including a series of features/points/trends/factors.

Analysis

Examine in detail to discover the meaning or essential features of a theme, topic or situation. Break something down into its components, examine factors methodically and in detail to recognise patterns by applying concepts and making connections to predict consequences.

Evaluation

Form an idea of the amount, number or value of someone or something. Examine in detail the meaning or essential features of a theme, topic or situation; break something down into its components; examine factors methodically and in detail, identify separate factors, say how they are related and how each one contributes to the topic to make reasoned judgements and conclusions.

91. Formatting a solicitor's letter

CPS – Crown prosecution service
HSE – Health and safety executive
QC – senior barrister
CJA – Criminal Justice Act
PACE – Police and Criminal Evidence Act

92. Writing a solicitor's letter to a client

A proactive approach is much preferred to a reactive approach after an accident has occurred. It is important that all health and safety policies and procedures are in place at your company and that staff are fully aware of the rules and regulations. Health and safety is extremely important to all organisations. HSE statistics show that '137 workers were killed at work' in 2016–2017 and, though few of these resulted from corporate manslaughter, deaths in the workplace are preventable.

After the Law Commission's recommendations in 1996 and campaigns by groups such as FACK (Families Against Corporate Killing), the Corporate Manslaughter and Corporate Homicide Act 2007 was introduced. The law was simplified, making it easier to establish corporate criminal liability, and since the Act came into force there have been a number of prosecutions mostly resulting in convictions.

I would be pleased to provide you with case law examples if required and should you have any further queries please do not hesitate to contact me.

Yours sincerely,

93. Applying the law: police powers

Jamal's arrest must be based on reasonable suspicion and necessity.

Jamal must be told he is under arrest and cautioned. He must be told the reason for the arrest and he must be taken to a police station as soon as reasonably practicable.

If Jamal is under 18 or vulnerable in some other way, a parent, guardian or carer must be contacted.

Jamal's detention will be recorded and checked by a custody officer in line with time clocks.

Jamal has a right to see the codes of practice and has a right to free, independent legal advice.

Jamal has a right to request that a relative or other person be informed of his whereabouts.

Jamal has a right to reasonable treatment in terms of rest, food and exercise.

Notes

Notes

Notes

Notes